THE ULTIMATE PRODUCTIVITY BLUEPRINT

THE ULTIMATE PRODUCTIVITY BLUEPRINT

10 Steps to Success

B. VINCENT

QuantumQuill Press

Contents

Chapter 1: Introduction to Productivity

Figuring out the Idea of Efficiency

In our speedy world, efficiency remains as a signal of productivity, directing people and associations towards accomplishing their objectives with accuracy and reason. At its center, efficiency embodies the craft of enhancing assets — time, energy, and exertion — to successfully deliver wanted results. It rises above simple hecticness, zeroing in rather on the essential allotment of assets to augment results.

To get a handle on the pith of efficiency, it's fundamental to dive into its multi-layered nature. Efficiency isn't exclusively about following through with jobs; it includes a comprehensive way to deal with work and life, enveloping elements like concentration, prioritization, and equilibrium. Whether it's gathering cutoff times, seeking after private interests, or driving authoritative development, efficiency fills in as the foundation of progress in each undertaking.

By understanding efficiency's subtleties, we engage ourselves to explore life's intricacies with clearness and reason. It's not just about accomplishing more; it's tied in with doing the right things in the absolute most productive way. As we leave on this excursion to unwind the secrets of efficiency, let us embrace its extraordinary power and release our maximum capacity to shape a future characterized by accomplishment and satisfaction.

The Brain research of Efficiency

Behind each useful activity lies an intricate interchange of considerations, feelings, and ways of behaving that shape our ability to really achieve undertakings. The brain research of efficiency digs into the internal functions of the human psyche, uncovering the mental cycles and profound elements that impact our capacity to remain on track, inspired, and on target.

At its embodiment, efficiency is as much about mentality for all intents and purposes about strategy. Our convictions, perspectives, and discernments assume a significant part in deciding our efficiency levels. A positive mentality, described by good faith, flexibility, and a development situated viewpoint, encourages a prolific ground for efficiency to thrive. On the other hand, negative idea designs, like self-uncertainty, compulsiveness, and apprehension about disappointment, can go about as considerable boundaries to advance.

Understanding the mental underpinnings of efficiency empowers us to successfully saddle our intellectual capacities more. Procedures like mental reevaluating, positive self-talk, and representation enable us to develop an outlook helpful for efficiency. By supporting a versatile and development situated outlook, we furnish ourselves with the psychological determination expected to conquer hindrances, persist notwithstanding difficulties, and keep up with force towards our objectives.

Also, digging into the domain of feelings divulges their significant effect on efficiency. Feelings, both good and pessimistic, act as powerful drivers of conduct, affecting our inspiration, direction, and in general prosperity. Figuring out how to deal with feelings capably — diverting them towards useful closures and alleviating their troublesome impacts — upgrades our ability to remain on track, versatile, and strong in the midst of life's horde requests.

As we disentangle the complicated functions of the human mind, we gain important experiences into the workmanship and study of efficiency. By sustaining a positive mentality, dominating our feelings, and developing mental flexibility, we open the maximum capacity of our psyches to accomplish more noteworthy degrees of efficiency and satisfaction in each part of our lives.

Normal Efficiency Traps

Chasing after efficiency, it's very simple to succumb to normal entanglements that ruin progress and wreck our best-laid plans. Perceiving and tending to these deterrents is fundamental for developing a strong and powerful way to deal with efficiency.

One pervasive trap is the charm of performing various tasks — a misleading practice that vows to help productivity yet frequently prompts decreased center and disappointing outcomes. Instead of shuffling various undertakings all the while, research recommends that solitary entrusting — giving our undivided focus to each assignment in turn — yields unrivaled results and improves generally speaking efficiency.

One more typical hindrance is hesitation, the inclination to postpone or stay away from undertakings regardless of knowing their significance. Tarrying can come from different sources, including dread of disappointment, hairsplitting, or essentially feeling overpowered by the greatness of an undertaking. Conquering lingering requires developing mindfulness, breaking assignments into reasonable advances, and embracing methodologies to defeat obstruction and cultivate energy.

Besides, deficient preparation and association can obstruct efficiency by encouraging confusion and failure. Without clear targets, focused on undertakings, and an organized way to deal with using time effectively, we risk becoming overpowered by the sheer volume of obligations, prompting pressure, burnout, and lessened efficiency.

Interruptions likewise represent a critical danger to efficiency in the present computerized age, where relentless warnings, messages, and online entertainment coax for our consideration. Figuring out how to oversee interruptions — whether by defining limits, laying out assigned work periods, or utilizing efficiency apparatuses — can assist with protecting our concentration and focus, permitting us to work with more noteworthy proficiency and viability.

Finally, an absence of self-control and responsibility can sabotage even the best goals for efficiency. Without the discipline to stick to plans, completely finish responsibilities, and consider ourselves responsible for our activities, we risk capitulating to inactivity and missing the mark concerning our objectives.

By recognizing these normal efficiency entanglements and executing systems to relieve their belongings, we strengthen our efficiency tool stash and make ready for supported achievement. Through mindfulness, proactive preparation, and trained execution, we engage ourselves to beat snags, remain fixed on our targets, and open our maximum capacity for efficiency and accomplishment.

Advantages of Being Useful

Embracing efficiency isn't only a necessary evil; an extraordinary excursion yields a horde of advantages across all features of life. By developing a proactive and deliberate way to deal with work and individual undertakings, we open an abundance of chances for development, satisfaction, and achievement.

One of the main advantages of efficiency is the capacity to accomplish more significantly quicker. By improving our assets — time, energy, and exertion — we enhance our viability and proficiency, empowering us to achieve errands with more prominent speed and accuracy. This elevated efficiency improves our result as well as saves important time for recreation, unwinding, and chasing after exercises that give us pleasure and satisfaction.

Besides, efficiency encourages a feeling of strengthening and command over our lives. By assuming responsibility for our time-tables, needs, and objectives, we state organization over our fate, as opposed to being helpless before outside conditions or passing interruptions. This feeling of independence imparts certainty, versatility, and a faith in our capacity to shape our ideal results — a mentality that fills further efficiency and accomplishment.

Moreover, efficiency breeds progress in both individual and expert domains. Whether it's progressing in our professions, sending off a business, or seeking after imaginative interests, a restrained and centered way to deal with efficiency positions us for more prominent open doors and achievements. By reliably conveying results and surpassing assumptions, we construct a standing for dependability, skill, and greatness — a standing that opens ways to additional opportunities and pushes us towards our yearnings.

Past substantial results, efficiency improves in general prosperity and personal satisfaction. By limiting pressure, overpower, and deep-seated insecurities, efficiency develops a feeling of satisfaction, fulfillment, and true serenity. It permits us to figure out some kind of harmony among work and recreation, empowering us to appreciate life's joys, support connections, and focus on taking care of oneself without culpability or split the difference.

At last, efficiency isn't simply an objective to be reached yet a ceaseless excursion of development, revelation, and discipline. By embracing its standards and receiving its complex rewards, we engage ourselves to lead deliberate, satisfying lives improved by accomplishment, importance, and euphoria.

Setting Clear Targets

At the core of any useful undertaking lies a reasonable feeling of direction and heading. Setting clear targets fills in as the compass that directs our activities, guaranteeing that we channel our time, energy, and assets towards significant and attainable objectives.

Lucidity is fundamental while characterizing goals. Questionable or dubious objectives can prompt disarray, hesitation, and an absence of inspiration. Along these lines, it's vital for articulate our targets with accuracy, determining what we expect to achieve, why it is important, and the way that we intend to accomplish it. This clearness hones our concentration as well as pervades our endeavors with reason and purposefulness.

Additionally, setting clear targets works with prioritization and navigation. At the point when we have a reasonable comprehension of our objectives, we can recognize which undertakings and exercises line up with our goals and merit our consideration. This lucidity engages us to dispense our time and assets reasonably, staying away from interruptions and zeroing in on exercises that draw us nearer to our ideal results.

Besides, clear targets give a structure to estimating progress and achievement. By laying out unambiguous achievements and benchmarks, we can follow our presentation, assess our adequacy, and make informed changes enroute. This criticism circle empowers us to course-right on a case by case basis, guaranteeing that we keep focused and stay lined up with our general goals.

Moreover, setting clear goals cultivates responsibility and inspiration. At the point when we openly focus on our objectives and offer them with others, we make a feeling of outside responsibility that moves us to finish our responsibilities. Besides, clear goals give a wellspring of inspiration, helping us to remember the reason behind our endeavors and moving us to persevere even with difficulties.

Basically, setting clear targets fills in as the foundation of efficiency, giving a guide to progress and a wellspring of inspiration and responsibility. By characterizing our goals with lucidity and purposefulness, we lay the preparation for accomplishing our desires and understanding our maximum capacity.

2

Chapter 2: Time Management Techniques

Prioritization and Time Blocking

In the bustling panorama of cutting-edge life, studying the artwork of prioritization and time blockading is crucial for navigating the myriad needs on our interest and energy. At its core, prioritization entails discerning between duties of various significance and urgency, making sure that we allocate our constrained time and sources to things to do that align with our overarching desires and objectives.

Effective prioritization starts off evolved with a clear perception of our dreams and objectives. By figuring out our most necessary duties and defining our priorities, we set up a roadmap for allocating our time and interest judiciously. This readability allows us to distinguish between duties that are necessary for development and these that are in simple terms distractions or reduced impact activities.

Once priorities are established, time blockading serves as a effective device for translating our intentions into action. Time blocking off entails putting apart devoted blocks of time for unique duties or activities, thereby developing centered durations of uninterrupted work. By allocating time deliberately and proactively, we defend in opposition to the encroachment of distractions and exterior interruptions, permitting us to dive deep into our work and make significant progress.

Moreover, time blocking off enables a feel of rhythm and shape in our every day routines. By scheduling duties in accordance to their degree of significance and our top intervals of focal point and energy, we optimize our productiveness and efficiency. This rhythmic method to time administration now not solely enhances our capability to accomplish duties however additionally cultivates a experience of stability and concord in our lives.

Furthermore, time blocking off empowers us to make deliberate preferences about how we spend our time. By consciously allocating time to things to do that align with our priorities and values, we assert manage over our schedules and shield towards the tyranny of the urgent. This intentional method to time administration fosters a experience of empowerment and autonomy, enabling us to format our days in a manner that displays our aspirations and aspirations.

In essence, prioritization and time blocking off serve as linchpins of high-quality time management, enabling us to center of attention our efforts on things to do that remember most and attain increased stages of productiveness and fulfillment. By getting to know these techniques, we liberate the conceivable to harness our time as a precious resource, directing it closer to interests that deliver us nearer to our desires and aspirations.

Pomodoro Technique

In the quest for greater productivity, the Pomodoro Technique emerges as a beacon of focal point amidst the chaos of cutting-edge distractions. Developed by means of Francesco Cirillo in the late 1980s, this time administration technique has garnered full-size acclaim for its simplicity and effectiveness in fostering attention and productivity.

At its core, the Pomodoro Technique revolves round the thought of working in short, centered bursts, interspersed with quick breaks. The method derives its title from the Italian phrase for "tomato," stimulated by way of the tomato-shaped kitchen timer that Cirillo originally used to song his work intervals. Each Pomodoro session commonly lasts for 25 minutes, observed by way of a quick 5-minute break. After finishing 4 Pomodoro sessions, a longer wreck of 15-30 minutes is taken to recharge and rejuvenate.

The splendor of the Pomodoro Technique lies in its capacity to harness the concepts of timeboxing and intermittent relaxation to optimize productiveness and keep sustained focus. By breaking duties into manageable intervals and placing a timer to music every session, we create a experience of urgency and accountability that propels us into a kingdom of flow—a intellectual kingdom characterized by way of deep awareness and gold standard performance.

Moreover, the Pomodoro Technique mitigates the perils of procrastination and burnout via introducing structured breaks at ordinary intervals. These quick respites serve as possibilities to rest, reset, and recharge, stopping intellectual fatigue and retaining cognitive sources for sustained productivity. Additionally, the Pomodoro Technique promotes mindfulness and self-awareness, as practitioners examine to tune into their electricity stages and regulate their work rhythms accordingly.

Furthermore, the Pomodoro Technique can be tailor-made to swimsuit man or woman preferences and work styles. While the normal Pomodoro interval is 25 minutes, some may additionally discover that shorter or longer classes higher swimsuit their needs.

Similarly, the length of breaks can be adjusted to accommodate non-public preferences and optimize productivity.

In essence, the Pomodoro Technique provides a easy but effective framework for improving focus, productivity, and normal well-being. By embracing this time-tested method, we reclaim manipulate over our interest and time, fostering a extra disciplined and intentional strategy to work and life. As we include the rhythm of the Pomodoro, we free up the doable to reap larger tiers of productiveness and achievement in our endeavors.

Parkinson's Law and Deadlines

Parkinson's Law, coined by means of British historian Cyril Northcote Parkinson in the 1950s, asserts that work expands to fill the time reachable for its completion. This profound perception into human conduct sheds mild on a imperative element of time management: the affect of cut-off dates on productivity.

At its essence, Parkinson's Law highlights the tendency for duties to increase in complexity and period when given unrestricted time frames. Without the constraint of deadlines, we frequently succumb to procrastination, permitting duties to linger on our to-do lists indefinitely. However, when confronted with approaching deadlines, we ride a surge of focus, motivation, and creativity, enabling us to accomplish duties with larger effectivity and effectiveness.

Harnessing the strength of Parkinson's Law includes putting synthetic time limits or time constraints to create a experience of urgency and momentum. By imposing time limits on tasks, we instill a feel of accountability and purpose, compelling us to prioritize our efforts and allocate assets judiciously. These self-imposed time limits serve as catalysts for action, using us to overcome inertia and make significant growth toward our goals.

Furthermore, Parkinson's Law underscores the significance of placing practical and plausible deadlines. While tight time limits can spur productivity, excessively formidable timelines might also backfire, main to stress, burnout, and compromised nice of work. Therefore, putting a stability between urgency and feasibility is necessary for leveraging the advantages of Parkinson's Law except succumbing to undue stress or unrealistic expectations.

Moreover, Parkinson's Law highlights the function of exterior cut-off dates in shaping our conduct and productivity. Whether imposed by way of clients, supervisors, or challenge milestones, exterior closing dates supply a experience of shape and accountability, guiding our movements and fostering collaboration and teamwork. By embracing exterior cut-off dates as possibilities for increase and achievement, we harness their motivational energy to propel us in the direction of success.

In essence, Parkinson's Law serves as a powerful reminder of the profound impact that cut-off dates wield over our productiveness and performance. By grasp and leveraging the standards of Parkinson's Law, we empower ourselves to harness the strength of cut-off dates to power focus, momentum, and success in our endeavors. As we embody the urgency of deadlines, we free up new degrees of productiveness and success, propelling us toward our desires with motive and determination.

Eliminating Time Wasters

In the quest for productivity, figuring out and removing time-wasting things to do is paramount. Time is a valuable and finite resource, and squandering it on unproductive endeavors can thwart our efforts to attain our dreams and aspirations. Therefore, it is necessary to undertake a discerning method to how we allocate our time and attention, rooting out distractions and inefficiencies that prevent our progress.

One frequent time-waster is immoderate multitasking—a pervasive dependency in modern day hyperconnected world. While multitasking may also appear like a shortcut to productivity, lookup suggests that it frequently leads to reduced focus, cognitive overload, and diminished performance. Instead of trying to juggle a couple of duties simultaneously, focusing on one project at a time approves us to channel our strength and interest extra effectively, yielding higher consequences in much less time.

Another common time-waster is succumbing to the charm of digital distractions. In an generation dominated by means of smartphones, social media, and infinite notifications, it is all too convenient to fall into the entice of senseless scrolling or compulsive electronic mail checking. These digital distractions now not solely eat treasured time however additionally disrupt our cognitive glide and lower our capacity to concentrate. By enforcing techniques to decrease digital distractions—such as turning off notifications, scheduling targeted instances for e mail and social media, and making use of internet site blockers—we reclaim manage over our interest and defend our focus.

Furthermore, inefficient workflows and tactics can additionally make contributions to wasted time and resources. Complex bureaucracies, redundant tasks, and inefficient verbal exchange channels can obstruct development and drain productivity. By streamlining workflows, automating repetitive tasks, and optimizing verbal exchange systems, we take away bottlenecks and inefficiencies, enabling us to work greater correctly and effectively.

Moreover, procrastination—a frequent foe of productivity—can siphon away valuable time if left unchecked. Procrastination frequently stems from fear, perfectionism, or overwhelm, main us to prolong necessary duties and prioritize non permanent gratification over long-term goals. Overcoming procrastination requires cultivating self-awareness, breaking duties into smaller, manageable steps, and imposing techniques to overcome resistance and inertia.

In essence, putting off time-wasters is fundamental for reclaiming manipulate over our time and maximizing our productiveness potential. By figuring out and addressing habits, distractions, and inefficiencies that sabotage our efforts, we create house for focused, purposeful action, enabling us to make substantial strides toward our dreams and aspirations. As we commit to ruthlessly removing time-wasters from our lives, we unencumber the ability to reap higher tiers of productivity, fulfillment, and success.

The Power of Saying No

In the pursuit of productivity, one of the most powerful but regularly unnoticed techniques is the artwork of announcing no. While it may also appear counterintuitive, getting to know to decline requests, commitments, and distractions that do no longer align with our priorities is crucial for safeguarding our time and energy, enabling us to focal point on what really matters.

Saying no is no longer about being impolite or uncooperative; rather, it is about placing boundaries, maintaining our priorities, and honoring our ability for significant contribution. By pronouncing no to activities, projects, or duties that do no longer align with our desires or values, we create area for the things to do that do, permitting us to make investments our time and electricity the place it will yield the biggest impact.

Moreover, pronouncing no is an act of self-care and self-preservation. In a world the place needs on our time and interest are incessant, pronouncing sure to the whole lot can lead to overwhelm, burnout, and a feel of depletion. By selectively pronouncing no to non-essential commitments, we defend our well-being, refill our reserves, and retain our capability for sustained productiveness and fulfillment.

Furthermore, announcing no cultivates readability and focus. When we say no to distractions, tangents, and extraneous commitments, we create a clear pathway for pursuing our dreams with single-minded determination. This readability permits us to allocate our time and assets greater effectively, making sure that we make development in the direction of our targets except undue detours or distractions.

Additionally, announcing no fosters admire and authenticity in our relationships. By placing boundaries and speaking our priorities overtly and honestly, we set up trust, integrity, and mutual appreciation with others. Saying no when critical demonstrates that we price our time and commitments, main to extra significant and productive interactions in the lengthy run.

In essence, the strength of pronouncing no lies in its capability to liberate us from the tyranny of busyness and obligation, empowering us to stay and work on our personal terms. By embracing the artwork of pronouncing no, we reclaim manage over our time, energy, and attention, enabling us to pursue our desires with clarity, purpose, and intentionality. As we study to wield the strength of no with grace and conviction, we free up the potential to acquire increased stages of productivity, fulfillment, and success in all areas of our lives.

3

Chapter 3: Goal Setting and Planning

SMART Goals Framework

In the ride closer to productiveness and success, putting desires is akin to charting a path for our aspirations. However, now not all dreams are created equal. To make sure that our goals are meaningful, achievable, and actionable, it is indispensable to undertake a framework that presents readability and structure. Enter the SMART desires framework—an valuable device for crafting dreams that are Specific, Measurable, Achievable, Relevant, and Time-bound.

Specificity is the cornerstone of advantageous aim setting. Rather than putting indistinct or ambiguous objectives, SMART desires demand precision and clarity, articulating precisely what we goal to accomplish and why it matters. By virtually defining our objectives, we get rid of ambiguity and furnish a clear route for our efforts, growing the possibility of success.

Measurability is imperative for monitoring growth and assessing outcomes. SMART desires are quantifiable, permitting us to gauge our overall performance objectively and measure our success towards predetermined metrics. Whether it is quantifying income targets, monitoring health milestones, or monitoring venture milestones, measurable dreams furnish tangible benchmarks for evaluating our development and course-correcting as needed.

Achievability ensures that our dreams are inside attain and aligned with our skills and resources. While it is essential to purpose high, putting unrealistic or unimaginable desires can lead to frustration and disillusionment. SMART desires strike a stability between ambition and feasibility, difficult us to stretch past our relief zones whilst closing grounded in reality.

Relevance ensures that our dreams are significant and aligned with our values, priorities, and long-term aspirations. SMART dreams resonate with our intrinsic motivations and serve as stepping stones toward our broader imaginative and prescient for success. By aligning our dreams with our passions and purpose, we infuse our efforts with which means and significance, growing our motivation and dedication to accomplishing them.

Lastly, time-bound desires introduce a experience of urgency and accountability, specifying a closing date or timeframe for completion. By putting clear timelines, we create a experience of momentum and focus, compelling us to take decisive motion and prioritize our efforts effectively. Moreover, time-bound desires stop procrastination and indecision, making sure that we make consistent development closer to our objectives.

In essence, the SMART desires framework presents a roadmap for remodeling aspirations into concrete moves and outcomes. By adopting this systematic strategy to aim setting, we empower ourselves to make clear our objectives, measure our progress, and navigate the course toward success with cause and intentionality. As we harness the electricity of SMART dreams to chart our course, we liberate the plausible to reap our most formidable goals and aspirations.

Creating Action Plans

Setting dreams is the first step toward realizing our dreams, however except a clear format of action, even the loftiest aspirations can stay elusive. Action plans serve as the bridge between our desires and their attainment, offering a roadmap that outlines the unique steps and techniques required to flip our imaginative and prescient into reality.

At its essence, growing an motion graph includes breaking down our dreams into manageable and actionable steps. Rather than viewing our targets as monolithic tasks, we deconstruct them into smaller, bite-sized movements that are less difficult to handle and track. This technique now not solely enhances readability and center of attention however additionally instills a feel of momentum and progress, as every carried out step brings us nearer to our remaining destination.

Moreover, motion plans supply a structured framework for organizing our efforts and sources effectively. By delineating tasks, deadlines, and responsibilities, we make certain that anyone worried is aligned and in charge for their contributions. This collaborative method fosters synergy and cohesion, enabling groups to work cohesively toward a frequent goal with readability and purpose.

Furthermore, motion plans serve as a device for overcoming barriers and mitigating risks. By looking ahead to practicable challenges and devising contingency plans, we proactively tackle setbacks and make certain that we stay adaptable and resilient in the face of adversity. This forward-thinking strategy empowers us to navigate uncertainty with confidence, understanding that we have a sketch in area to climate any storm that may additionally arise.

Additionally, motion plans grant a mechanism for monitoring development and monitoring performance. By organizing clear milestones and benchmarks, we can measure our development and course-correct as wished to continue to be on track. This ongoing comparison allows us to perceive areas for improvement, capitalize on opportunities, and have a good time milestones alongside the way.

In essence, developing motion plans is the linchpin of high-quality intention implementation and execution. By translating our aspirations into actionable steps and strategies, we radically change summary desires into concrete realities. As we embark on the trip outlined in our motion plans, we unleash our doable to gain greatness, one step at a time.

Long-term vs. Short-term Goals

In the pursuit of productiveness and private growth, placing a stability between long-term aspirations and temporary goals is paramount. While long-term dreams grant a North Star to information our trip and anchor our ambitions, non permanent desires serve as incremental stepping stones that propel us ahead and hold our momentum.

Long-term desires symbolize the pinnacle of our aspirations— the remaining vacation spot closer to which we strive. These over-arching targets paint a vivid image of the future we envision for ourselves, inspiring us to dream large and purpose high. Whether it is attaining profession success, reaching economic independence, or cultivating significant relationships, long-term desires grant a feel of reason and route that infuses our efforts with that means and significance.

However, whilst long-term desires supply a compelling imag-inative and prescient for the future, they can additionally appear daunting and overwhelming in their magnitude. This is the place non permanent desires come into play. Short-term dreams wreck down our long-term aspirations into manageable and actionable steps, enabling us to make development incrementally and construct momentum over time.

Short-term desires are the constructing blocks of success—the small wins and achievements that preserve us influenced and targeted on our journey. Whether it is finishing a challenge milestone, obtaining a new skill, or setting up a every day habit, non permanent desires grant tangible proof of growth and toughen our dedication to our long-term objectives. Moreover, accomplishing non permanent dreams boosts our self assurance and self-efficacy, empowering us to address increasingly more bold challenges with dedication and resilience.

Furthermore, non permanent dreams supply flexibility and adaptability in our pursuit of long-term success. As we navigate life's twists and turns, our priorities and instances can also evolve, requiring us to alter our route accordingly. Short-term dreams permit us to pivot and recalibrate our trajectory as needed, making sure that we stay agile and responsive to altering prerequisites except dropping sight of our final destination.

In essence, the interaction between long-term and non permanent desires varieties the cornerstone of fine purpose putting and planning. By balancing visionary aspirations with pragmatic motion steps, we create a roadmap for success that is each inspiring and achievable. As we harness the energy of each non permanent and long-term goals, we liberate the possible to realize our desires and aspirations with clarity, purpose, and determination.

Visualizing Success

In the pursuit of our goals, harnessing the energy of visualization can be a mighty device for bettering motivation, focus, and aim attainment. Visualization, additionally regarded as intellectual imagery or intellectual rehearsal, entails vividly imagining ourselves reaching our desires and experiencing the feelings related with success. By attractive our senses and feelings in this intellectual rehearsal, we top our minds and our bodies for height performance, aligning our ideas and moves with our preferred outcomes.

Visualizing success serves various key functions in the goal-setting process. First and foremost, it clarifies our intentions and desires, assisting us to crystallize our dreams and aspirations with increased precision and clarity. When we visualize ourselves reaching our goals, we faucet into our unconscious mind's innate ability to appear our desires, programming it with a clear blueprint for success.

Moreover, visualization prompts the motivational facilities of our brain, igniting a feel of passion, purpose, and willpower inside us. When we vividly think about ourselves reaching our goals—feeling the excitement of success, the pride of accomplishment, and the satisfaction of achievement—we gasoline our motivation and dedication to take motion in the direction of realizing our dreams.

Furthermore, visualization cultivates a mind-set of abundance and possibility, transferring our center of attention from obstacles to opportunities. By envisioning ourselves overcoming obstacles, persevering thru challenges, and finally attaining success, we instill a experience of resilience and optimism that empowers us to persist in the face of adversity.

Additionally, visualization enhances our overall performance with the aid of programming our minds and our bodies for success. Numerous research have tested the efficacy of intellectual rehearsal in enhancing skills, boosting confidence, and improving overall performance throughout a range of domains, from sports activities and lecturers to commercial enterprise and private development. By mentally rehearsing our movements and outcomes, we create neural pathways that give a boost to our competencies and make bigger our possibility of success when we stumble upon real-world challenges.

In essence, visualization is a effective device for aligning our thoughts, emotions, and moves with our dreams and aspirations. By harnessing the energy of visualization, we spark off the full conceivable of our minds and bodies, paving the way for larger stages of achievement, fulfillment, and success. As we immerse ourselves in the wealthy tapestry of our desires and aspirations thru visualization, we release the ability to flip our visions into fact with unwavering conviction and determination.

Reviewing and Adjusting Goals

In the dynamic experience of purpose pursuit, it is fundamental to apprehend that desires are no longer set in stone however instead bendy and adaptable to altering occasions and priorities. As we development toward our objectives, it's integral to typically overview our goals, examine our progress, and make crucial changes to make sure that we stay aligned with our imaginative and prescient and aspirations.

Regularly reviewing our desires offers an chance for reflection and introspection, permitting us to consider our modern trajectory and become aware of any gaps or discrepancies between our favored consequences and our authentic progress. By taking inventory of our achievements, challenges, and training learned, we achieve precious insights into what's working nicely and the place changes may additionally be wished to continue to be on course.

Moreover, reviewing our dreams allows us to have fun our successes and well known our accomplishments, no depend how small. Celebrating milestones no longer solely boosts our morale and motivation however additionally reinforces our dedication to our goals, fueling our force to proceed striving for excellence and progress.

Furthermore, reviewing our dreams fosters accountability and possession of our outcomes. When we usually determine our development and maintain ourselves answerable for our actions, we domesticate a experience of accountability and employer in attaining our objectives. This accountability empowers us to take proactive steps toward our goals, as a substitute than passively ready for success to happen.

In addition to reviewing our goals, it's quintessential to be open to adjusting them as needed. Circumstances change, priorities shift, and sudden barriers may additionally occur alongside the way. Flexibility and adaptability are key virtues in intention pursuit, permitting us to pivot and course-correct as wanted to continue to be on tune in the direction of our preferred outcomes.

Adjusting dreams entails re-evaluating our objectives, refining our strategies, and putting new aims or timelines as necessary. This iterative manner of refinement and realignment ensures that our desires continue to be relevant, achievable, and in alignment with our evolving aspirations and circumstances.

In essence, reviewing and adjusting desires is a essential issue of high quality intention putting and planning. By preserving a non-stop comments loop of reflection, assessment, and adjustment, we make certain that our desires continue to be dynamic, responsive, and attuned to our ever-changing environment. As we embody this iterative method to intention pursuit, we empower ourselves to navigate the complexities of lifestyles with resilience, adaptability, and unwavering dedication to our desires and aspirations.

4

Chapter 4: Organization Strategies

Decluttering and Streamlining

In the bustling panorama of current life, decluttering and streamlining our bodily and digital environments emerge as vital practices for fostering productivity, clarity, and peace of mind. Clutter—whether tangible or virtual—can act as a barrier to efficiency, sapping our electricity and focal point and hindering our potential to accomplish duties effectively.

Decluttering starts off evolved with a aware evaluation of our surroundings, whether or not it is our bodily workspace or digital devices. It includes figuring out items, documents, or digital documents that no longer serve a reason or make contributions to our productiveness desires and making intentional choices about their disposition. By decluttering our environments, we create bodily and intellectual house for the things to do and endeavors that virtually matter, permitting us to work with higher focus, clarity, and purpose.

Moreover, decluttering extends past mere tidying up; it is additionally about simplifying and optimizing our workflows and processes. This may additionally contain getting rid of redundant tasks, consolidating statistics and resources, and developing streamlined structures for managing our responsibilities. By lowering complexity and inefficiency in our workflows, we decorate our productiveness and effectiveness, enabling us to accomplish extra with much less effort and stress.

In the digital realm, decluttering entails organizing and curating our digital spaces—whether it is our electronic mail inbox, laptop desktop, or digital documents and folders. Digital muddle can be simply as dangerous to productiveness as bodily clutter, inundating us with distractions and making it tough to discover imperative data when needed. By imposing techniques for organizing and managing digital assets—such as developing folders, the usage of labels and tags, and often archiving or deleting old-fashioned files—we optimize our digital environments for productiveness and efficiency.

Furthermore, decluttering is now not a one-time match however instead an ongoing exercise that requires diligence and commitment. Just as muddle accumulates steadily over time, so too need to we persistently declutter and streamline our environments to hold their effectiveness and functionality. By integrating decluttering into our everyday routines and habits, we domesticate a lifestyle of simplicity, order, and productiveness that permeates each element of our lives.

In essence, decluttering and streamlining are foundational practices for growing environments that aid productivity, focus, and well-being. By simplifying our surroundings, we free ourselves from the distractions and burdens of extra and create house for clarity, creativity, and growth. As we embody the ideas of decluttering and streamlining, we pave the way for higher efficiency, effectiveness, and achievement in all areas of our lives.

Time Management Tools

In the fast-paced world we inhabit, studying time administration is necessary for navigating the myriad needs on our interest and energy. Fortunately, a plethora of equipment and apps exist to assist us prepare our schedules, prioritize tasks, and maximize productivity. From typical planners and calendars to modern digital solutions, these time administration equipment offer a vary of points and functionalities to go well with numerous preferences and needs.

At the coronary heart of high quality time administration equipment is the potential to centralize and arrange our duties and commitments in one reachable location. Whether it is a bodily planner or a digital assignment administration app, having a centralized hub permits us to capture, track, and prioritize our to-do lists with ease, making sure that nothing falls via the cracks and that we remain targeted on what things most.

Moreover, time administration equipment facilitate high quality planning and scheduling by way of offering equipment for placing deadlines, growing reminders, and allocating time blocks for precise duties and activities. By breaking down our day into manageable chunks and assigning committed time slots to every task, we beautify our focal point and productivity, making constant growth closer to our goals.

Furthermore, many time administration equipment provide elements for collaboration and communication, enabling groups to coordinate and delegate duties efficiently. Whether it is shared calendars, collaborative challenge administration platforms, or verbal exchange equipment with built-in mission administration functionalities, these equipment streamline workflows and foster collaboration, making sure that each person stays on the equal web page and that tasks pass ahead smoothly.

Additionally, time administration equipment frequently come geared up with analytics and reporting facets that permit us to song our progress, perceive patterns, and analyze our productiveness habits. By gaining insights into how we spend our time and the place we can improve, we can make knowledgeable selections about how to optimize our workflows and allocate our sources extra effectively.

In essence, time administration equipment are fundamental belongings in our quest for productiveness and efficiency. By harnessing the energy of these equipment to arrange our schedules, prioritize tasks, and streamline workflows, we empower ourselves to make the most of our time and reap our dreams with increased clarity, focus, and effectiveness. As we leverage the skills of time administration equipment to their fullest extent, we release the achievable to lead greater balanced, fulfilling, and purpose-driven lives.

Prioritization Techniques

In the fast-paced world we inhabit, gaining knowledge of the artwork of prioritization is integral for navigating the consistent barrage of duties and obligations that compete for our attention. Prioritization entails discerning between duties of various significance and urgency, making sure that we allocate our restrained time and assets to things to do that align with our dreams and objectives.

One fine prioritization method is the Eisenhower Matrix, named after former U.S. President Dwight D. Eisenhower, who famously said, "What is necessary is seldom urgent, and what is pressing is seldom important." The Eisenhower Matrix categorizes duties into 4 quadrants based totally on their stage of urgency and importance: essential and urgent, essential however no longer urgent, pressing however no longer important, and neither pressing nor important. By categorizing duties in this manner, we can center of attention our efforts on things to do that have the best have an effect on our desires whilst minimizing time spent on low-value or trivial tasks.

Another prioritization method is the ABCDE method, popularized by way of Brian Tracy in his e book "Eat That Frog!" This technique entails assigning precedence tiers (A, B, C, D, or E) to every undertaking based totally on its significance and urgency. Tasks special as A are pinnacle priorities and have to be accomplished immediately, whilst duties labeled as B are essential however now not pressing and can be scheduled for later. C duties are nice-to-have however now not critical, whilst D duties can be delegated to others. Finally, E duties are duties that can be eradicated altogether, as they do no longer make a contribution to our dreams or priorities.

Additionally, the Pareto Principle, additionally regarded as the 80/20 rule, is a treasured device for prioritization. This precept states that roughly 80% of consequences come from 20% of efforts. By figuring out the small variety of duties or things to do that yield the best consequences and focusing our efforts on them, we can maximize our productiveness and gain larger effects with much less time and effort.

Furthermore, the MoSCoW method, many times used in task management, categorizes necessities or duties into 4 categories: Must have, Should have, Could have, and Won't have. By prioritizing duties based totally on these categories, groups can make sure that vital necessities are addressed first, observed via much less crucial gadgets as sources allow.

In essence, studying prioritization methods is crucial for maximizing productiveness and attaining our desires with readability and focus. By adopting techniques such as the Eisenhower Matrix, ABCDE method, Pareto Principle, and MoSCoW method, we can make sure that we allocate our time and sources strategically, focusing on things to do that align with our targets and pressure significant progress. As we prioritize our efforts effectively, we release the attainable to accomplish greater with less, main to higher pride and achievement in each our non-public and expert lives.

Creating Systems and Routines

In the pursuit of productiveness and efficiency, developing structured structures and routines is paramount. Systems and routines furnish a framework for organizing our tasks, managing our time, and streamlining our workflows, enabling us to work with larger focus, consistency, and effectiveness.

At its core, growing structures entails creating standardized procedures and processes for performing duties and coping with responsibilities. By setting up clear pointers and protocols, we minimize ambiguity and uncertainty, making sure that anyone concerned is aware of what is predicted of them and how to execute their roles efficiently. This consistency and predictability foster a experience of order and reliability, minimizing blunders and delays whilst maximizing productiveness and effectiveness.

Moreover, structures assist us leverage automation and delegation to optimize our workflows and preserve our time and power for higher-value activities. By figuring out repetitive duties and creating computerized options or delegating them to others, we free ourselves from the drudgery of guide labor and focal point on duties that require our special competencies and expertise. This strategic allocation of assets enhances our productiveness and permits us to accomplish extra in much less time.

Additionally, routines play a indispensable position in preserving consistency and momentum in our each day lives. Routines furnish shape and stability, grounding us in a rhythm that fosters self-discipline and productivity. Whether it is a morning hobbies to begin the day on the proper foot, a work movements to hold focal point and productiveness all through the day, or an night events to wind down and put together for rest, routines assist us domesticate habits and rituals that help our well-being and success.

Furthermore, structures and routines promote accountability and development monitoring by means of supplying checkpoints and milestones for evaluating our overall performance and course-correcting as needed. By integrating comments mechanisms into our structures and routines, we can display our progress, discover areas for improvement, and make changes to make sure that we remain on music toward our goals.

In essence, growing structures and routines is about designing our lives in a way that maximizes efficiency, effectiveness, and fulfillment. By imposing structured processes, automating repetitive tasks, and setting up steady routines, we create an surroundings that helps our productiveness and success, enabling us to attain our dreams with clarity, focus, and purpose. As we include the electricity of structures and routines, we release the attainable to lead greater organized, balanced, and satisfying lives.

Optimizing Workspace

A well-organized and optimized workspace is a cornerstone of productiveness and focus. Our bodily and digital work environments profoundly affect our potential to concentrate, collaborate, and create. Therefore, investing time and effort into designing and organizing our workspace can yield sizable dividends in phrases of efficiency, creativity, and normal well-being.

Begin by using decluttering and tidying your bodily workspace. Remove needless items, file away paperwork, and make certain that fundamental equipment and components are without difficulty accessible. A clutter-free surroundings fosters readability of thinking and minimizes distractions, permitting you to pay attention on the project at hand besides needless interruptions.

Consider the ergonomics of your workspace to promote alleviation and forestall stress or injury. Ensure that your desk and chair are adjusted to assist suitable posture, and make investments in ergonomic add-ons such as a keyboard tray or reveal stand if necessary. A blissful and ergonomic workspace enhances productiveness and reduces fatigue, enabling you to work greater effortlessly and efficaciously for prolonged periods.

Organize your digital workspace with equal care and attention. Declutter your pc desktop, prepare documents and folders logically, and put into effect a regular naming conference to facilitate effortless retrieval of archives and information. Use productiveness equipment such as digital calendars, undertaking administration apps, and note-taking software program to hold tune of deadlines, prioritize tasks, and seize thoughts and insights as they arise.

Design your workspace to encourage creativity and focus. Personalize your surroundings with significant decorations, artwork, or vegetation that evoke a experience of calm and inspiration. Consider incorporating factors of nature, such as herbal light, greenery, or views of the outdoors, which have been proven to enhance mood, creativity, and productivity.

Finally, optimize your workspace for collaboration and verbal exchange if you work in a group environment. Create specific areas for meetings, brainstorming sessions, and collaborative work, geared up with equipment and applied sciences that facilitate conversation and collaboration, such as whiteboards, video conferencing equipment, and assignment administration software.

In essence, optimizing your workspace is about developing an surroundings that helps your productivity, creativity, and well-being. By decluttering, organizing, and personalizing your bodily and digital workspaces, you create a conducive surroundings for focused, efficient, and stimulated work. As you make investments in optimizing your workspace, you lay the basis for larger productivity, satisfaction, and success in your endeavors.

5

Chapter 5: Motivation and Discipline

Understanding Motivation

Motivation is the riding pressure at the back of our thoughts, emotions, and actions, shaping our conduct and influencing our pursuit of desires and aspirations. Understanding the complicated interaction of psychological elements that underpin motivation is imperative for harnessing its electricity to gasoline our productiveness and success.

At its core, motivation is fueled by way of a mixture of intrinsic and extrinsic factors. Intrinsic motivation arises from within, pushed through our innate desires, interests, and values. It is the inner hearth that propels us to pursue things to do for their very own sake, deriving pride and achievement from the method itself. Extrinsic motivation, on the different hand, comes from exterior sources such as rewards, recognition, or social approval. While extrinsic rewards can furnish brief incentives to interact in positive behaviors, they are regularly much less sustainable and might also undermine intrinsic motivation if overemphasized.

Various theories and fashions have been proposed to give an explanation for the mechanisms of motivation, every shedding mild on unique factors of human behavior. From Maslow's Hierarchy of Needs, which posits that people are inspired by way of a hierarchy of desires ranging from physiological to self-actualization, to Self-Determination Theory, which emphasizes the significance of autonomy, competence, and relatedness in riding intrinsic motivation, these frameworks grant treasured insights into the complicated nature of motivation.

Moreover, perception man or woman variations in motivation is fundamental for tailoring techniques and interventions to successfully interact and encourage people. Some men and women may additionally be pushed via a sturdy experience of reason or intrinsic ardor for their work, whilst others may additionally reply extra positively to exterior incentives or tangible rewards. By recognizing and respecting these differences, we can create environments and incentives that maximize motivation and engagement for all.

Furthermore, motivation is now not static however dynamic, fluctuating in response to modifications in our environment, circumstances, and inner states. Factors such as stress, fatigue, or lack of readability can dampen motivation, whilst supportive relationships, significant goals, and a feel of development can reignite it. By cultivating self-awareness and monitoring our motivation levels, we can proactively tackle boundaries and leverage possibilities to maintain our pressure and momentum.

In essence, grasp motivation is a multifaceted pastime that requires perception into the interaction of interior and exterior factors, character differences, and the dynamic nature of human behavior. By delving into the complexities of motivation, we release the achievable to encourage and empower ourselves and others to attain our fullest plausible and recognize our most formidable goals and aspirations.

Cultivating Intrinsic Motivation

Intrinsic motivation, frequently viewed the purest shape of motivation, arises from inside and is pushed by means of our innate desires, interests, and values. Unlike extrinsic motivation, which depends on exterior rewards or incentives, intrinsic motivation stems from a actual enjoyment of the undertaking itself and the pleasure derived from getting to know new skills, pursuing private interests, or reaching self-directed goals.

Cultivating intrinsic motivation includes tapping into our passions, strengths, and feel of autonomy to gas our engagement and dedication to our endeavors. One tremendous method for nurturing intrinsic motivation is to align our things to do with our core values and interests. When we have interaction in things to do that resonate with our values and passions, we trip a feel of motive and achievement that energizes and sustains our efforts over the lengthy term.

Another key aspect in cultivating intrinsic motivation is fostering a experience of autonomy and self-determination. Providing persons with possibilities to make choices, set goals, and exercising manage over their moves empowers them to take possession of their work and fosters a experience of business enterprise and responsibility. This autonomy now not solely enhances intrinsic motivation however additionally promotes creativity, innovation, and self-expression.

Furthermore, fostering a increase mindset—one that embraces challenges, values effort, and views setbacks as possibilities for studying and growth—is instrumental in cultivating intrinsic motivation. When we undertake a boom mindset, we embody the trust that our skills and talent can be developed via dedication and effort, as an alternative than being constant or predetermined. This mind-set fosters resilience, perseverance, and a willingness to take on new challenges, all of which are crucial for sustaining intrinsic motivation in the face of limitations and setbacks.

Moreover, presenting opportunities for mastery and talent improvement is necessary for nurturing intrinsic motivation. When we have interaction in things to do that enable us to increase and refine our skills, we ride a experience of competence and mastery that fuels our motivation and drive. Whether it is mastering a new instrument, gaining knowledge of a new language, or honing our expert skills, the pursuit of mastery offers a effective supply of intrinsic motivation and fulfillment.

In essence, cultivating intrinsic motivation includes fostering a deep feel of passion, purpose, and autonomy in our pursuits. By aligning our things to do with our values and interests, offering possibilities for autonomy and self-determination, fostering a increase mindset, and merchandising possibilities for mastery, we create an surroundings that nurtures intrinsic motivation and empowers humans to pursue their dreams with passion, purpose, and perseverance. As we domesticate intrinsic motivation in ourselves and others, we liberate the achievable for sustained engagement, creativity, and achievement in all elements of our lives.

Harnessing External Motivation

While intrinsic motivation is frequently viewed the perfect using pressure at the back of sustained engagement and commitment, exterior motivation additionally performs a substantial function in fueling our moves and behaviors. External motivators, such as rewards, recognition, and accountability mechanisms, can grant precious incentives to bolster motivation and keep momentum, especially in conditions the place intrinsic motivation may additionally be missing or insufficient.

One way to harness external motivation successfully is via the use of rewards and incentives. Whether it is monetary bonuses, performance-based incentives, or tangible rewards such as presents or prizes, exterior rewards can serve as effective motivators to inspire preferred behaviors and outcomes. By linking rewards to particular dreams or milestones, we create a feel of urgency and motivation to reap them, using people to exert effort and persevere in the face of challenges.

Moreover, focus and reward can be strong sources of exterior motivation, validating individuals' efforts and accomplishments and reinforcing favored behaviors. Whether it is a easy phrase of grasp from a colleague or formal focus in the front of peers, acknowledgment of one's contributions and achievements can increase morale, decorate self-esteem, and gasoline motivation to proceed performing at a excessive level.

Additionally, accountability mechanisms can serve as exterior motivators to promote consistency and self-discipline in our actions. Whether it is placing public goals, sharing growth updates with a mentor or accountability partner, or collaborating in accountability organizations or challenges, exterior accountability affords a built-in aid gadget that holds us responsible for our commitments and encourages us to continue to be centered and disciplined in pursuit of our goals.

Furthermore, social incentives, such as peer pressure, competition, or social norms, can additionally serve as effective exterior motivators to force conduct alternate and inspire adherence to preferred norms and standards. By leveraging the electricity of social influence, we can faucet into individuals' innate wish for acceptance and belonging to inspire them to align their moves with shared dreams and values.

In essence, whilst intrinsic motivation is absolutely precious for fostering sustained engagement and commitment, exterior motivation additionally has a quintessential function to play in using conduct exchange and attaining preferred outcomes. By harnessing the energy of rewards, recognition, accountability mechanisms, and social incentives, we can create a supportive surroundings that motivates people to function at their pleasant and acquire their dreams with clarity, focus, and determination. As we leverage exterior motivation effectively, we unencumber the attainable for better performance, productivity, and success in all elements of our lives.

Building Discipline

Discipline is the cornerstone of fulfillment and success, imparting the basis for steady action, resilience in the face of adversity, and the potential to continue to be centered on long-term goals. While motivation might also furnish the preliminary spark to get started, it is self-discipline that sustains momentum and incorporates us via the inevitable challenges and setbacks alongside the way.

Building self-discipline entails cultivating habits and routines that aid our dreams and priorities, even when confronted with distractions, temptations, or obstacles. One high-quality approach for constructing self-discipline is to set up clear desires and motion plans, breaking down large targets into smaller, manageable duties and committing to a normal agenda for their completion. By putting specific, measurable, and conceivable goals, we grant ourselves with clear pursuits to intention for and a roadmap to information our actions.

Moreover, developing accountability mechanisms can assist support self-discipline and dedication to our goals. Whether it is sharing our desires with a depended on buddy or mentor, becoming a member of a supportive neighborhood or accountability group, or the usage of monitoring equipment and apps to display progress, exterior accountability gives an introduced layer of motivation and encouragement to continue to be disciplined and targeted on our objectives.

Additionally, practicing strength of will and delayed gratification is quintessential for constructing discipline. This entails resisting the impulse to indulge in on the spot pleasures or distractions in prefer of long-term rewards and benefits. By cultivating the capability to prolong gratification and continue to be centered on our priorities, we fortify our strength of mind muscle and beautify our ability to persevere via challenges and setbacks.

Furthermore, growing a supportive surroundings that minimizes distractions and fosters focal point is indispensable for constructing discipline. This might also contain putting boundaries round our time and space, limiting publicity to distractions such as social media or television, and developing a devoted workspace that is conducive to attention and productivity. By optimizing our surroundings for success, we limit the possibility of succumbing to temptation and make bigger our capability to continue to be disciplined and targeted on our goals.

In essence, constructing self-discipline is a lifelong experience that requires commitment, effort, and perseverance. By organizing clear goals, developing accountability mechanisms, working towards strength of will and delayed gratification, and developing a supportive environment, we enhance our self-discipline muscle and amplify our capability to gain our desires with clarity, focus, and determination. As we domesticate self-discipline in our lives, we release the plausible for sustained success, fulfillment, and non-public growth.

Sustaining Motivation Through Challenges

Maintaining motivation at some point of difficult instances is quintessential for staying on direction closer to our dreams and aspirations. However, adversity, setbacks, and uncertainty can check even the strongest resolve, making it difficult to maintain motivation and momentum. Nevertheless, there are techniques and strategies we can hire to navigate these challenges and preserve our motivation alive.

One high quality method for sustaining motivation for the

duration of tough instances is to domesticate resilience—the potential to jump again from setbacks, adapt to change, and persevere in the face of adversity. Resilience is now not about keeping off challenges or screw ups however alternatively about embracing them as possibilities for increase and learning. By reframing setbacks as precious studying experiences and focusing on the training they offer, we can hold a wonderful outlook and hold shifting ahead no matter obstacles.

Moreover, retaining a increase mindset—a faith that our skills and talent can be developed via dedication and effort—can bolster our resilience and maintain motivation in the course of difficult times. When we view challenges as possibilities to stretch and grow, as a substitute than insurmountable obstacles, we method them with a experience of optimism and determination, understanding that we have the capability to overcome them via perseverance and effort.

Additionally, practicing self-care and prioritizing well-being is imperative for sustaining motivation all through difficult times. Taking care of our physical, mental, and emotional fitness permits us to recharge our batteries, control stress extra effectively, and preserve a high quality mindset. Whether it is via everyday exercise, mindfulness practices, enough sleep, or in search of assist from buddies and cherished ones, investing in self-care replenishes our strength reserves and strengthens our resilience in the face of adversity.

Furthermore, staying linked to our feel of motive and imaginative and prescient can furnish a supply of thought and motivation at some stage in challenging times. By reconnecting with our underlying motives for pursuing our dreams and aspirations, we faucet into a deep properly of intrinsic motivation that sustains us via challenges and setbacks. Whether it is our wish to make a high quality impact, acquire non-public growth, or fulfill our potential, anchoring ourselves in our experience of motive reminds us of what absolutely things and fuels our dedication to persevere.

In essence, sustaining motivation via challenges requires resilience, a boom mindset, self-care, and a connection to our experience of purpose. By cultivating these characteristics and practices, we can navigate tough instances with resilience, optimism, and determination, staying targeted on our dreams and aspirations even in the face of adversity. As we climate life's storms and emerge more suitable on the different side, we unencumber the doable for growth, resilience, and success in our non-public and expert lives.

6

Chapter 6: Energy Management

Understanding Energy Levels

Energy ranges are the foreign money of productiveness and well-being, influencing our capacity to function tasks, make decisions, and interact with the world round us. Understanding the dynamics of strength degrees is fundamental for optimizing our overall performance and keeping stability in our lives.

At its core, strength is no longer simply a bodily phenomenon however a multifaceted thought that encompasses physical, mental, and emotional dimensions. Physical electricity refers to the vitality and stamina required to raise out bodily duties and activities, whilst intellectual strength pertains to cognitive features such as focus, concentration, and problem-solving. Emotional energy, on the different hand, relates to our emotional well-being and resilience in the face of stress and challenges.

Managing our power correctly entails recognizing the interaction between these one-of-a-kind dimensions and figuring out techniques to fill up and maintain them over time. Just as a financial institution account requires deposits and withdrawals to keep a wholesome balance, so too does our strength device require durations of recreation and relaxation to feature optimally.

Moreover, power tiers fluctuate at some stage in the day in response to a number of elements such as sleep, nutrition, stress, and bodily activity. By tuning into our body's herbal rhythms and appreciation our character electricity patterns, we can agenda duties and things to do to align with our height strength levels, maximizing productiveness and performance.

Furthermore, power administration is no longer simply about conserving power however additionally about replenishing it thru practices that promote renewal and rejuvenation. This might also contain enticing in things to do that recharge us physically, mentally, and emotionally, such as exercise, meditation, hobbies, or spending time with cherished ones. By incorporating these practices into our day by day routines, we can preserve our strength ranges over the lengthy time period and forestall burnout and fatigue.

In essence, perception electricity tiers is crucial for optimizing productivity, performance, and well-being. By recognizing the interaction between physical, mental, and emotional electricity and enforcing techniques to control and refill our power effectively, we can acquire higher balance, vitality, and achievement in all elements of our lives. As we prioritize strength administration as a cornerstone of our each day habits and routines, we release the possible to thrive with clarity, focus, and resilience.

Maximizing Physical Energy

Physical electricity types the basis of our vitality and normal well-being, influencing our ability to interact in each day activities, keep focus, and manipulate stress. Maximizing bodily power entails adopting habits and practices that aid foremost fitness and vitality, enabling us to maintain strength stages all through the day and operate at our best.

One key factor of maximizing bodily strength is prioritizing sleep and rest. Adequate sleep is critical for bodily recovery, cognitive function, and emotional resilience. Aim for 7-9 hours of first-class sleep every night, setting up a constant bedtime pursuits and growing a sleep-friendly surroundings free from distractions. Additionally, incorporating quick breaks and durations of relaxation at some stage in the day can assist stop fatigue and refill strength levels, permitting you to preserve focal point and productivity.

Nutrition additionally performs a essential position in maximizing bodily energy. Fuel your physique with a balanced weight loss plan prosperous in fruits, vegetables, entire grains, lean proteins, and wholesome fat to furnish sustained electricity all through the day. Avoid immoderate consumption of processed foods, sugary snacks, and caffeine, as these can lead to electricity crashes and fluctuations in blood sugar levels. Stay hydrated by way of ingesting lots of water during the day, as dehydration can impair cognitive feature and scale back power levels.

Regular bodily pastime is any other crucial thing of maximizing bodily energy. Exercise no longer solely strengthens the physique and improves cardiovascular fitness however additionally boosts mood, enhances cognitive function, and will increase power levels. Aim for at least 30 minutes of moderate-intensity workout most days of the week, incorporating a combine of aerobic, energy training, and flexibility workout routines to promote standard fitness and vitality.

Moreover, managing stress is indispensable for keeping bodily strength and stopping burnout. Practice stress-reduction strategies such as deep breathing, meditation, yoga, or mindfulness to promote leisure and resilience in the face of stressors. Prioritize things to do that convey you pleasure and fulfillment, and examine to set boundaries to shield your bodily and emotional well-being.

In essence, maximizing bodily power includes adopting habits and practices that guide most excellent sleep, nutrition, exercise, and stress management. By prioritizing self-care and investing in your bodily fitness and vitality, you can preserve electricity levels, beautify productivity, and thrive with vitality and resilience in all components of your life. As you domesticate habits that promote bodily energy, you release the attainable to stay lifestyles to the fullest, with clarity, vitality, and purpose.

Cultivating Mental Energy

Mental strength is the gas that powers our cognitive functions, which includes focus, concentration, memory, and problem-solving abilities. Cultivating intellectual electricity includes adopting techniques and practices that beautify cognitive function, promote mental clarity, and preserve center of attention and productiveness during the day.

One superb method for cultivating intellectual power is to prioritize duties and things to do that align with your height cognitive periods. Identify instances of the day when you experience most alert, focused, and mentally sharp, and time table your most difficult or worrying duties in the course of these periods. By capitalizing on your herbal electricity rhythms, you can maximize productiveness and efficiency, tackling complicated duties when your cognitive assets are at their peak.

Additionally, managing distractions is critical for maintaining intellectual electricity and retaining focus. Minimize interruptions and distractions in your surroundings with the aid of developing a committed workspace free from noise, clutter, and pointless stimuli. Use equipment and strategies such as time-blocking, the Pomodoro Technique, or digital distractions blockers to reduce interruptions and create centered blocks of time for deep work and concentration.

Furthermore, working towards mindfulness and cognitive techniques can assist sharpen intellectual acuity and decorate cognitive function. Incorporate mindfulness practices such as meditation, deep respiration exercises, or aware focus into your every day hobbies to domesticate higher attentional control, emotional regulation, and intellectual clarity. Additionally, interact in things to do that undertaking your cognitive abilities, such as puzzles, intelligence games, or studying new skills, to hold your thought sharp and agile.

Moreover, managing cognitive load and intellectual fatigue is imperative for keeping intellectual power and stopping burnout. Break duties down into smaller, extra manageable components, and keep away from overloading your working reminiscence with too a good deal records at once. Take everyday breaks for the duration of the day to relaxation and recharge, permitting your idea to get better and rejuvenate between intervals of excessive concentration.

In essence, cultivating intellectual strength includes adopting techniques and practices that beautify cognitive function, promote intellectual clarity, and maintain center of attention and productivity. By aligning duties with your height cognitive periods, managing distractions, working towards mindfulness, and managing cognitive load, you can optimize your intellectual strength and function at your best, reaching higher clarity, focus, and productiveness in all factors of your life. As you domesticate habits that aid intellectual energy, you liberate the attainable to suppose greater clearly, make higher decisions, and reap your desires with larger ease and effectiveness.

Nurturing Emotional Energy

Emotional strength is the gas that powers our resilience, optimism, and standard well-being, influencing our potential to navigate challenges, control stress, and preserve a effective outlook on life. Nurturing emotional strength includes adopting practices and techniques that promote emotional resilience, domesticate positivity, and foster a experience of well-being amidst life's ups and downs.

One indispensable component of nurturing emotional electricity is training self-awareness and emotional regulation. Take time to tune into your emotions, become aware of underlying ideas and beliefs, and renowned and validate your emotions barring judgment. Practice self-compassion and self-care, treating your self with kindness and appreciation at some stage in hard times, and creating wholesome coping mechanisms for managing stress and adversity.

Moreover, fostering significant connections and relationships is indispensable for nurturing emotional strength and promotion a experience of belonging and support. Cultivate relationships with friends, family, and colleagues who uplift and encourage you, and prioritize satisfactory time spent together. Engage in things to do that foster connection and camaraderie, such as social gatherings, shared hobbies, or significant conversations, to nourish your emotional well-being and beef up your social guide network.

Furthermore, discovering cause and that means in existence is imperative for nurturing emotional power and fostering a experience of success and satisfaction. Identify your core values, passions, and aspirations, and align your movements with your feel of cause to create a experience of that means and path in your life. Engage in things to do that deliver you joy, fulfillment, and a experience of accomplishment, whether or not it is pursuing a hobby, volunteering for a reason you accept as true with in, or putting and working toward significant goals.

Additionally, working towards gratitude and cultivating a advantageous mind-set can help nurture emotional electricity and foster resilience in the face of adversity. Take time every day to replicate on the matters you are grateful for, focusing on the positives in your existence instead than living on the negatives. Adopt a increase mindset, viewing challenges as possibilities for boom and learning, and reframing setbacks as precious classes that toughen your resilience and character.

In essence, nurturing emotional power includes cultivating self-awareness, fostering significant connections, discovering motive and meaning, and training gratitude and positivity. By prioritizing emotional well-being and investing in practices that promote resilience, optimism, and fulfillment, you can nourish your emotional strength and thrive amidst life's challenges and uncertainties. As you domesticate habits that aid emotional energy, you free up the conceivable to stay with higher joy, resilience, and authenticity, embracing life's ups and downs with grace and resilience.

Balancing Energy Expenditure and Renewal

Achieving superior power administration includes placing a refined stability between expending electricity via things to do and renewing power thru relaxation and rejuvenation. Just as a battery requires each discharge and recharge cycles to feature effectively, so too do our bodies and minds want a stability of exercise and relaxation to hold height overall performance and well-being.

One key element of balancing electricity expenditure and renewal is recognizing the significance of pacing and rhythm in our each day lives. Avoid overcommitting your self or taking on too many duties at once, as this can lead to burnout and depletion of electricity reserves. Instead, prioritize duties and things to do based totally on their significance and urgency, and allocate time for breaks and durations of relaxation in the course of the day to recharge and fill up your power levels.

Moreover, comprise practices and rituals that promote relaxation and rejuvenation into your each day routine. Set apart time for things to do that carry you pleasure and relaxation, such as spending time in nature, working towards mindfulness or meditation, or attractive in innovative pursuits. Prioritize sleep and create a restful sleep surroundings conducive to deep, restorative rest, making sure that you get the first-rate and extent of sleep wanted to recharge your strength reserves.

Furthermore, hear to your body's indicators and honor your herbal electricity rhythms. Pay interest to signs and symptoms of fatigue, stress, or burnout, and take proactive steps to tackle them via scaling returned on activities, looking for support, or enforcing self-care practices. Tune into your body's cues for hunger, thirst, and movement, and reply consequently to hold stability and vitality.

Additionally, exercise electricity administration on a broader scale by way of periodically assessing and adjusting your commitments and priorities to make sure alignment with your values and goals. Regularly assessment your time table and workload, and become aware of areas the place you can delegate tasks, streamline processes, or say no to extra obligations to stop crush and keep stability in your life.

In essence, balancing strength expenditure and renewal is critical for sustaining height performance, productivity, and well-being. By prioritizing relaxation and rejuvenation, listening to your body's signals, and managing your commitments and priorities effectively, you can preserve a healthful stability between pastime and rest, enabling you to thrive with clarity, vitality, and resilience in all components of your life. As you domesticate habits that aid electricity balance, you unencumber the workable to stay with higher purpose, fulfillment, and joy, embracing life's challenges and possibilities with grace and resilience.

7

Chapter 7: Effective Communication

Understanding the Importance of Communication

Communication serves as the cornerstone of human interaction, taking part in a pivotal function in fostering connection, understanding, and collaboration in each non-public and expert contexts. At its core, wonderful verbal exchange is the artwork of conveying ideas, thoughts, and feelings in a clear, concise, and compelling manner, whilst additionally actively listening and empathizing with others to foster mutual appreciation and respect.

In private relationships, conversation varieties the bedrock of intimacy, trust, and emotional connection. Open and straightforward conversation approves people to specific their feelings, needs, and desires, fostering empathy, validation, and aid from their partners. Conversely, a lack of verbal exchange or ineffective conversation can lead to misunderstandings, conflicts, and resentment, eroding the basis of have faith and intimacy in relationships.

In the expert realm, advantageous verbal exchange is equally integral for riding productivity, collaboration, and success. Clear and concise verbal exchange ensures that crew participants apprehend their roles, responsibilities, and objectives, aligning efforts closer to frequent desires and objectives. Moreover, advantageous conversation fosters a way of life of transparency, openness, and have confidence inside organizations, enabling leaders to inspire, motivate, and interact their groups effectively.

Furthermore, fine verbal exchange is necessary for navigating complicated interpersonal dynamics, managing conflicts, and constructing strong, cohesive teams. By fostering open dialogue, energetic listening, and empathy, people can tackle variations constructively, get to the bottom of conflicts amicably, and domesticate a lifestyle of respect, inclusion, and collaboration inside their groups and organizations.

Moreover, advantageous conversation extends past verbal exchanges to embody nonverbal cues, physique language, and tone of voice. Nonverbal verbal exchange debts for a sizeable component of the message conveyed, influencing how our phrases are perceived and interpreted by using others. By being aware of nonverbal cues and physique language, humans can beautify the clarity, impact, and effectiveness of their communication, fostering higher grasp and connection with others.

In essence, perception the significance of verbal exchange is vital for constructing and preserving healthy, gratifying relationships, each individually and professionally. By prioritizing clear, empathetic conversation and actively listening to others, people can foster understanding, trust, and collaboration, laying the groundwork for success and success in all elements of life. As we apprehend conversation as a essential talent to domesticate and refine, we liberate the practicable to deepen our connections, foster tremendous relationships, and reap our dreams with clarity, confidence, and grace.

Active Listening and Empathy

Active listening and empathy are foundational elements of nice communication, enabling men and women to join deeply with others, construct trust, and foster understanding. Active listening includes completely attractive with the speaker, no longer solely listening to their phrases however additionally paying interest to their tone, physique language, and emotions, whilst empathy includes perception and sharing the emotions and views of others.

One key thing of lively listening is giving the speaker your full interest and being absolutely current in the moment. This capacity placing apart distractions, such as digital gadgets or interior thoughts, and focusing on the speaker's phrases and nonverbal cues. Maintain eye contact, nod in acknowledgment, and use verbal cues such as "I see," "Go on," or "Tell me more" to sign your activity and inspire the speaker to proceed sharing.

Moreover, exercise reflective listening with the aid of paraphrasing or summarizing the speaker's phrases to make sure grasp and display empathy. Reflective listening includes restating the speaker's message in your very own words, shooting the essence of what they've stated and acknowledging their emotions and perspectives. This no longer solely validates the speaker's experiences however additionally fosters a deeper experience of connection and perception between each parties.

Furthermore, domesticate empathy by using placing your self in the different person's footwear and searching for to recognize their thoughts, feelings, and experiences from their perspective. Empathy includes tuning into the emotional undercurrents of the conversation, recognizing and validating the speaker's emotions, and responding with compassion and understanding. Avoid judgment or criticism and as a substitute center of attention on expressing empathy and assist for the speaker's experiences.

Additionally, ask open-ended questions and inspire the speaker to complex on their ideas and feelings, fostering deeper exploration and grasp of their perspective. Avoid interrupting or speeding to provide solutions, as this can undermine the speaker's experience of business enterprise and autonomy. Instead, enable the speaker to specific themselves absolutely and hear barring judgment, developing a secure and supportive house for open communicate and mutual understanding.

In essence, lively listening and empathy are crucial abilities for constructing strong, significant relationships and fostering nice communication. By practicing lively listening, reflective listening, and empathy, humans can join greater deeply with others, construct trust, and domesticate a tradition of perception and collaboration. As we prioritize these capabilities in our interactions, we release the possible to construct stronger, extra gratifying relationships and navigate life's challenges with empathy, compassion, and grace.

Clarity and Conciseness

Clarity and conciseness are integral standards of tremendous communication, making sure that messages are conveyed accurately, succinctly, and comprehensively. Clear conversation entails expressing ideas, thoughts, and data in a manner that is without problems understood through the meant audience, whilst conciseness entails conveying facts succinctly and besides useless elaboration or complexity.

One critical factor of readability in verbal exchange is the usage of easy and simple language that is available to the meant audience. Avoid jargon, technical terminology, or complicated language that can also confuse or alienate the listener. Instead, attempt for readability by means of the usage of simple language and concrete examples to illustrate your points, making it less difficult for others to recognize and interact with your message.

Moreover, furnish context and history data to make certain that your message is clear and understandable to the recipient. This may additionally contain summarizing key points, supplying applicable heritage information, or clarifying any phrases or standards that can also be unfamiliar to the listener. By imparting context and clarification, you assist make certain that your message is understood in the meant way and decrease the danger of misunderstandings or misinterpretations.

Furthermore, be concise in your conversation by using getting to the factor shortly and fending off pointless verbosity or tangents. Respect the listener's time and interest by way of handing over your message succinctly and efficiently, focusing on the most integral factors and omitting needless important points or filler. Use bullet points, lists, or headings to prepare your ideas and bring data in a clear and concise manner, making it simpler for the recipient to draw close the key takeaways.

Additionally, be conscious of the medium and structure of your verbal exchange and tailor your message accordingly. Whether speaking verbally, in writing, or via digital channels, adapt your message to swimsuit the context and preferences of the recipient. Use excellent formatting, tone, and fashion to carry your message effectively, taking into account cultural differences, language proficiency, and verbal exchange norms.

In essence, readability and conciseness are necessary for fine communication, making sure that messages are understood precisely and efficiently. By prioritizing simplicity, imparting context, and being concise in your communication, you can deliver your message surely and comprehensively, fostering grasp and engagement with your audience. As we domesticate readability and conciseness in our communication, we unencumber the practicable to construct better relationships, foster collaboration, and gain our dreams with readability and precision.

Assertiveness and Diplomacy

Assertiveness and diplomacy are necessary elements of high-quality communication, enabling humans to specific their thoughts, opinions, and desires confidently and respectfully whilst retaining superb relationships and fostering mutual understanding. Assertiveness entails advocating for oneself in a clear, direct, and assured manner, whilst diplomacy entails navigating interpersonal interactions with tact, sensitivity, and consideration for others' perspectives.

One key element of assertive conversation is expressing oneself brazenly and in reality whilst respecting the rights and boundaries of others. Assertive people talk their thoughts, feelings, and wishes at once and assertively, except resorting to passive-aggressive conduct or manipulation. They categorical themselves confidently and assertively, the use of "I" statements to take possession of their ideas and emotions and averting blaming or accusing others.

Moreover, assertive conversation includes putting clear boundaries and assertively putting forward one's rights and preferences in interpersonal interactions. Assertive people are capable to say "no" when vital and assert their boundaries firmly and respectfully, barring feeling responsible or apologizing excessively. They assert themselves confidently and assertively, advocating for their desires and priorities whilst respecting the rights and views of others.

Furthermore, diplomacy is critical for navigating complicated interpersonal dynamics and managing conflicts effectively. Diplomatic men and women talk with tact, sensitivity, and empathy, thinking about the emotions and views of others whilst expressing their very own ideas and opinions. They pick out their phrases carefully, keeping off harsh or confrontational language, and are searching for to get to the bottom of conflicts amicably thru open communicate and negotiation.

Additionally, diplomatic conversation includes lively listening and empathy, looking for to apprehend others' views and issues earlier than expressing one's personal ideas and opinions. Diplomatic people renowned and validate the emotions and views of others, even when they disagree, and attempt to discover frequent floor and areas of compromise. They foster mutual recognize and appreciation thru open speak and positive communication, constructing stronger, greater resilient relationships in the process.

In essence, assertiveness and diplomacy are crucial abilities for superb communication, enabling men and women to specific themselves confidently and respectfully whilst keeping effective relationships and fostering mutual understanding. By cultivating assertiveness and diplomacy in our communication, we can navigate interpersonal interactions with self belief and grace, fostering trust, respect, and collaboration in all elements of our lives. As we prioritize these competencies in our interactions, we free up the achievable to construct stronger, extra gratifying relationships and attain our dreams with clarity, confidence, and integrity.

Nonverbal Communication and Body Language

Nonverbal verbal exchange and physique language play a indispensable position in tremendous communication, influencing how messages are perceived and interpreted through others. While verbal exchange conveys the content material of our message, nonverbal cues such as facial expressions, gestures, posture, and tone of voice grant extra layers of meaning, shaping the general have an effect on and reception of our communication.

One key thing of nonverbal conversation is being conscious of your very own physique language and nonverbal cues when speaking with others. Pay interest to your facial expressions, posture, and gestures, as these can bring emotions, attitudes, and intentions greater powerfully than phrases alone. Maintain open and comfy physique language, make eye contact, and use gestures and facial expressions to emphasize key factors and deliver sincerity and authenticity.

Moreover, be attuned to the nonverbal cues and physique language of others at some stage in communication, as these can furnish treasured insights into their thoughts, feelings, and intentions. Notice refined adjustments in facial expressions, physique posture, and tone of voice, as these can also point out underlying thoughts or reactions that are now not expressed verbally. By tuning into nonverbal cues, you can higher recognize the real that means and context of the conversation and reply appropriately.

Furthermore, use nonverbal cues consciously to decorate the clarity, impact, and effectiveness of your communication. Match your nonverbal cues to your verbal message to make sure consistency and toughen your meant meaning. For example, keep eye contact when speaking to bring self belief and sincerity, use gestures to illustrate key points, and regulate your tone of voice and facial expressions to replicate the emotional tone of your message.

Additionally, be conscious of cultural variations and norms involving nonverbal communication, as these may additionally range broadly throughout specific cultures and contexts. What may additionally be viewed gorgeous or wonderful nonverbal verbal exchange in one tradition might also be perceived in another way in another. Respect cultural variations and adapt your nonverbal verbal exchange fashion thus to make certain mutual grasp and appreciate in cross-cultural interactions.

In essence, nonverbal verbal exchange and physique language are effective equipment for improving the clarity, impact, and effectiveness of communication. By being aware of your personal nonverbal cues, attuned to the nonverbal cues of others, and the usage of nonverbal verbal exchange consciously and appropriately, you can foster deeper understanding, connection, and rapport in your interpersonal interactions. As we domesticate consciousness and mastery of nonverbal communication, we liberate the attainable to talk with higher clarity, influence, and effectiveness, constructing stronger, greater significant relationships in the process.

8

Chapter 8: Continuous Learning and Growth

The Importance of Lifelong Learning

Lifelong mastering stands as an fundamental cornerstone in each private and expert growth, serving as a perpetual experience of self-discovery, talent enhancement, and mental expansion. Embracing non-stop studying nurtures a mind-set of curiosity and adaptability, enabling men and women to navigate the ever-evolving panorama of know-how and innovation with self belief and agility.

In the realm of non-public development, lifelong getting to know empowers persons to develop their horizons, deepen their appreciation of the world, and domesticate new passions and interests. Whether thru formal education, self-directed study, or experiential learning, the pursuit of information fosters mental curiosity and enriches lifestyles experiences, fueling non-public increase and fulfillment.

Professionally, the cost of lifelong mastering can't be overstated in modern day dynamic and aggressive job market. Rapid technological developments and evolving enterprise developments demand that specialists always replace their capabilities and know-how to continue to be applicable and competitive. Embracing lifelong getting to know equips humans with the adaptability and resilience wanted to thrive in their careers, catch new opportunities, and continue to be in advance of the curve in an ever-changing landscape.

Moreover, lifelong getting to know serves as a catalyst for innovation and creativity, riding progress and development throughout all sectors and industries. By fostering a tradition of curiosity, experimentation, and non-stop improvement, businesses can harness the collective skills and insights of their group of workers to power innovation, clear up complicated problems, and obtain sustainable boom and success.

Furthermore, lifelong studying promotes non-public empowerment and self-actualization, empowering men and women to take possession of their non-public and expert improvement and chart their very own paths to success. By embracing a boom attitude and committing to lifelong learning, humans can release their full potential, overcome challenges, and attain their dreams with self belief and determination.

In essence, lifelong studying is now not basically a skill to an quit however a trip of self-discovery, growth, and empowerment. By embracing non-stop gaining knowledge of and growth, people can enrich their lives, enhance their careers, and make significant contributions to society, embodying the timeless pursuit of know-how and the boundless conceivable of the human spirit. As we include lifelong studying as a guiding principle, we release the achievable to lead fulfilling, purpose-driven lives and make a lasting have an effect on the world round us.

Cultivating a Growth Mindset

Cultivating a increase attitude is foundational to embracing the experience of non-stop studying and growth. At its core, a increase attitude is a trust machine that revolves round the appreciation that intelligence, abilities, and skills are no longer constant characteristics however can be developed and extended via dedication, effort, and perseverance. Embracing a boom attitude empowers humans to include challenges, view disasters as possibilities for mastering and growth, and persist in the face of setbacks with resilience and determination.

One fundamental issue of cultivating a boom mind-set is reframing setbacks and disasters as possibilities for mastering and development. Instead of viewing failure as a reflection of their competencies or worth, men and women with a increase mind-set see it as a herbal phase of the studying process—a danger to discover areas for improvement, refine their skills, and finally develop superior and greater capable. By embracing failure as a stepping stone to success as an alternative than a roadblock, people with a increase attitude method challenges with braveness and optimism, understanding that every setback brings them one step nearer to their goals.

Moreover, cultivating a increase attitude includes embracing challenges as possibilities for increase and expansion. Rather than shying away from situation or discomfort, folks with a boom mind-set actively searching for out challenges that push them outdoor their remedy sector and stretch their abilities. They method new experiences with curiosity and enthusiasm, viewing barriers as possibilities to learn, adapt, and evolve. By embracing challenges with a boom mindset, folks can unencumber their full potential, find out new skills and abilities, and acquire breakthroughs that propel them to new heights of success and fulfillment.

Furthermore, creating a increase attitude requires fostering a experience of resilience and perseverance in the face of adversity. Individuals with a increase attitude apprehend that success is now not constantly linear and that setbacks and limitations are inevitable on the direction to mastery. Instead of giving up when confronted with challenges or setbacks, they persevere with willpower and grit, the usage of setbacks as gas to propel them ahead as an alternative than boundaries to maintain them back. By cultivating resilience and perseverance, persons with a boom attitude can overcome obstacles, navigate setbacks, and subsequently attain their dreams with resilience and determination.

Additionally, cultivating a increase mind-set includes embracing the strength of yet—the trust that with time, effort, and practice, persons can enhance and gain their goals. Instead of viewing their capabilities as constant and immutable, people with a increase mind-set undertake a attitude of non-stop enhancement and growth, recognizing that development is feasible with dedication and persistence. By embracing the electricity of yet, men and women can strategy challenges with a feel of optimism and possibility, understanding that with time and effort, they can reap their dreams and fulfill their potential.

In essence, cultivating a boom attitude is imperative for embracing the trip of non-stop getting to know and growth. By reframing setbacks as possibilities for learning, embracing challenges with resilience and determination, and adopting a attitude of non-stop improvement, humans can unencumber their full potential, acquire their goals, and thrive in each their non-public and expert lives. As we domesticate a boom mindset, we release the attainable to overcome obstacles, catch opportunities, and create a existence of purpose, passion, and fulfillment.

Setting Learning Goals

Setting mastering dreams is a essential step in the trip of non-stop getting to know and growth, presenting direction, motivation, and focal point to one's private and expert improvement efforts. Learning desires serve as roadmaps for character progress, guiding humans closer to obtaining new knowledge, growing skills, and accomplishing favored effects in a systematic and intentional manner.

One fundamental element of putting gaining knowledge of desires is making sure that they are specific, measurable, achievable, relevant, and time-bound (SMART). Specific desires grant readability and center of attention by way of surely defining what men and women purpose to achieve, whilst measurable dreams enable for monitoring growth and assessing success objectively. Achievable desires are practical and possible inside a given timeframe, whilst applicable desires align with individuals' values, aspirations, and priorities. Lastly, time-bound dreams set up clear time limits or milestones for achievement, presenting a experience of urgency and accountability.

Moreover, when putting gaining knowledge of goals, people need to reflect on consideration on their non-public and expert aspirations, strengths, and areas for growth. Reflecting on one's values, interests, and long-term targets can assist humans discover significant getting to know desires that align with their overarching imaginative and prescient for success and fulfillment. By putting dreams that resonate with their passions and aspirations, persons can keep motivation and enthusiasm for their getting to know journey, even in the face of challenges or setbacks.

Furthermore, breaking down large mastering desires into smaller, manageable duties or milestones can make them extra conceivable and actionable. By dividing mastering goals into bite-sized chunks and setting up a step-by-step graph for achievement, persons can make development incrementally and construct momentum in the direction of their large goals. This strategy additionally permits for flexibility and adaptability, as men and women can modify their gaining knowledge of plans primarily based on feedback, altering priorities, or unexpected circumstances.

Additionally, accountability mechanisms such as ordinary

growth reviews, checkpoints, or accountability companions can assist people continue to be on music and keep momentum closer to their getting to know goals. Sharing desires with others, looking for remarks and support, and celebrating milestones alongside the way can grant motivation and encouragement, fostering a experience of accountability and dedication to one's gaining knowledge of journey.

In essence, placing gaining knowledge of dreams is critical for guiding and motivating men and women in their pursuit of non-stop gaining knowledge of and growth. By organizing SMART dreams that are specific, measurable, achievable, relevant, and time-bound, persons can create a roadmap for their private and expert development, aligning their efforts with their aspirations and values. As we set and pursue mastering dreams with intention and determination, we free up the workable to enlarge our knowledge, advance new skills, and gain our full potential, each for my part and professionally.

Embracing Feedback and Iteration

Embracing comments and generation is a vital issue of the non-stop mastering process, enabling humans to refine their skills, deepen their understanding, and develop each individually and professionally. Feedback—whether effective or constructive—provides precious insights into one's performance, providing views and possibilities for enhancement that may additionally now not be right away apparent. By embracing remarks with an open thinking and a willingness to learn, humans can leverage it as a catalyst for increase and development.

One fundamental thing of embracing remarks is growing a life-style of openness, trust, and psychological protection inside private and expert environments. When men and women experience protected and supported in giving and receiving feedback, they are greater possibly to interact in sincere and positive dialogue, share insights and perspectives, and collaborate efficaciously closer to frequent goals. By fostering a lifestyle of feedback, businesses and groups can promote non-stop learning, innovation, and improvement, using collective success and growth.

Moreover, receiving comments gracefully and with humility is vital for maximizing its fee and impact. Instead of turning into protective or dismissive in the face of criticism, humans have to method comments with curiosity and a increase mindset, searching for to recognize and examine from the views of others. Actively listening to feedback, asking clarifying questions, and reflecting on its implications can assist folks reap precious insights, perceive areas for improvement, and develop professionally and personally.

Furthermore, soliciting remarks from various sources and views can supply a extra complete appreciation of one's strengths, weaknesses, and possibilities for growth. Seeking remarks from peers, mentors, supervisors, and stakeholders approves folks to attain one of a kind views and insights, fostering a deeper appreciation of their overall performance and impact. By soliciting remarks proactively and regularly, persons can perceive blind spots, tackle areas for improvement, and speed up their getting to know and improvement journey.

Additionally, incorporating comments into an iterative getting to know system includes making use of insights and tips to refine and enhance one's skills, strategies, and processes over time. Instead of viewing remarks as a one-time event, people must see it as an ongoing procedure of refinement and optimization, always looking for possibilities to learn, grow, and evolve. By iterating on remarks and incorporating classes discovered into future movements and decisions, persons can decorate their performance, attain higher success, and understand their full potential.

In essence, embracing remarks and new release is indispensable for fostering non-stop getting to know and growth, each in my opinion and professionally. By developing a subculture of openness, trust, and psychological safety, receiving remarks gracefully, soliciting numerous perspectives, and incorporating comments into an iterative getting to know process, men and women can harness the strength of remarks to pressure improvement, innovation, and success. As we include comments as a catalyst for boom and development, we unencumber the doable to reap our goals, fulfill our potential, and make significant contributions to the world round us.

Creating a Learning Culture

Creating a mastering way of life inside groups and businesses is paramount to fostering non-stop studying and boom at each the man or woman and collective levels. A studying way of life is characterized by using a shared dedication to curiosity, experimentation, expertise sharing, and non-stop improvement, the place studying is valued, encouraged, and built-in into the material of day by day operations and interactions.

One imperative component of growing a mastering subculture is promotion know-how sharing and collaboration amongst group members. By developing possibilities for folks to share their expertise, insights, and experiences with one another, agencies can faucet into the collective knowledge and creativity of their workforce, fostering innovation, problem-solving, and cross-functional collaboration. Knowledge sharing platforms, peer gaining knowledge of groups, and mentorship packages are simply a few examples of initiatives that can facilitate information change and foster a tradition of non-stop mastering inside organizations.

Moreover, leaders play a indispensable position in shaping and nurturing a gaining knowledge of lifestyle inside their groups and organizations. By modeling a dedication to mastering and growth, leaders encourage and empower their groups to prioritize studying as an integral aspect of success. Leaders can create area for mastering through offering resources, support, and possibilities for expert development, and by way of recognizing and lucrative people who display a dedication to gaining knowledge of and improvement. By championing a gaining knowledge of attitude and main by using example, leaders can domesticate a tradition the place curiosity, innovation, and boom are celebrated and encouraged.

Furthermore, embedding studying into the cloth of organizational tactics and structures is integral for growing a sustainable getting to know culture. By integrating studying possibilities into overall performance management, brain development, and strategic planning processes, companies can make certain that getting to know is prioritized and supported at all levels. This can also involve incorporating studying goals into overall performance goals, presenting devoted time and assets for education and development, and aligning mastering initiatives with organizational desires and priorities. By making mastering an imperative section of the organizational DNA, businesses can foster a lifestyle of non-stop enhancement and innovation that drives success and resilience in the face of change.

Additionally, fostering a studying tradition entails growing psychological protection and believe inside groups and organizations, the place persons sense satisfied taking risks, asking questions, and experimenting with new thoughts and approaches. When men and women sense secure to voice their opinions, share their ideas, and make mistakes barring worry of judgment or reprisal, they are greater in all likelihood to interact in open dialogue, discover new possibilities, and innovate with confidence. Cultivating psychological security requires leaders to domesticate an surroundings of trust, respect, and inclusivity, the place various views are valued and all voices are heard and respected.

In essence, developing a studying lifestyle is crucial for fostering non-stop gaining knowledge of and boom inside groups and organizations. By promotion understanding sharing, encouraging experimentation, and integrating getting to know into organizational procedures and systems, groups can domesticate a lifestyle the place curiosity, innovation, and boom thrive. As we include getting to know as a core price and prioritize its integration into our day by day operations and interactions, we unencumber the doable to gain larger success, resilience, and fulfillment, each for my part and collectively.

9

Chapter 9: Resilience and Overcoming Obstacles

Understanding Resilience

Resilience, regularly considered as the cornerstone of emotional and intellectual strength, is the potential to stand up to and rebound from adversity with fortitude, adaptability, and perseverance. It embodies a dynamic system of going through life's challenges, setbacks, and hardships with resilience, embracing them as possibilities for growth, learning, and transformation alternatively than insurmountable barriers. Understanding resilience entails recognizing the multifaceted nature of adversity and the myriad approaches in which people reply to and navigate tough circumstances.

At its core, resilience includes the capability to continue to be steadfast in the face of adversity, keeping a experience of optimism, hope, and willpower even in the midst of uncertainty and difficulty. It encompasses the ability to adjust one's emotions, manipulate stress, and cope efficiently with adversity, drawing upon inner and exterior assets to navigate challenges with grace and resilience. Moreover, resilience is no longer in basic terms about bouncing lower back to one's preceding nation however about bouncing forward, rising from adversity stronger, wiser, and greater resilient than before.

Furthermore, resilience entails cultivating a increase mindset—an mind-set of curiosity, openness, and resilience toward challenges and setbacks. Individuals with a increase attitude view barriers as possibilities for increase and learning, reframing setbacks as transient setbacks as an alternative than everlasting roadblocks. They include challenges with resilience, perseverance, and a trust in their capacity to overcome adversity, recognizing that resilience is now not a constant trait however a talent that can be developed and bolstered over time.

Additionally, grasp resilience requires recognizing the significance of social support, connections, and relationships in bolstering resilience at some point of instances of adversity. Strong social networks supply a source of emotional support, encouragement, and perspective, enabling people to navigate challenges with resilience and confidence. By fostering significant connections and nurturing supportive relationships, humans can construct a basis of resilience that sustains them thru life's inevitable ups and downs.

In essence, perception resilience is crucial for navigating life's challenges, setbacks, and adversities with strength, grace, and perseverance. By cultivating a increase mindset, harnessing social guide networks, and embracing challenges as possibilities for growth, persons can domesticate resilience as a core capability that empowers them to thrive in the face of adversity. As we deepen our appreciation of resilience and domesticate its traits inside ourselves, we unencumber the achievable to navigate life's challenges with resilience, courage, and resilience.

Building Resilience Skills

Building resilience abilities is fundamental for equipping folks with the equipment and techniques wanted to navigate life's challenges, setbacks, and adversities with strength, adaptability, and perseverance. Resilience capabilities embody a extensive vary of cognitive, emotional, and behavioral talents that allow humans to efficiently cope with stress, manipulate adversity, and leap lower back from setbacks with resilience and determination.

One critical resilience talent is emotional regulation—the capability to recognize, understand, and manipulate one's thoughts in wholesome and optimistic ways. Emotionally resilient folks are adept at figuring out and expressing their feelings, regulating extreme thoughts such as fear, anger, or sadness, and keeping emotional stability and balance even in the face of adversity. They domesticate self-awareness and mindfulness, working towards methods such as deep breathing, meditation, and rest workouts to manipulate stress and promote emotional well-being.

Moreover, problem-solving capabilities are fundamental for constructing resilience, as they allow people to strategy challenges and setbacks with a proactive and solution-focused mindset. Resilient folks are expert problem-solvers, adept at figuring out obstacles, producing innovative solutions, and enforcing tremendous techniques to overcome adversity. They strategy challenges with optimism, resourcefulness, and a willingness to take calculated risks, viewing setbacks as possibilities for boom and gaining knowledge of as a substitute than insurmountable barriers.

Additionally, resilience entails creating advantageous coping mechanisms to navigate stress, adversity, and uncertainty with grace and resilience. Coping abilities such as in search of social support, working towards self-care, and enticing in things to do that promote rest and well-being are vital for constructing resilience and keeping intellectual and emotional fitness all through difficult times. Resilient persons prioritize self-care and prioritize things to do that nourish their mind, body, and spirit, recognizing that caring for oneself is crucial for constructing resilience and sustaining well-being.

Furthermore, resilience abilities consist of cultivating adaptive wondering patterns and beliefs that promote resilience and optimism in the face of adversity. Resilient folks possess a increase mindset—an mindset of curiosity, openness, and resilience in the direction of challenges and setbacks. They view barriers as possibilities for increase and learning, reframing setbacks as transient setbacks as a substitute than everlasting failures. By cultivating a boom mindset, persons can harness the strength of resilience to navigate challenges with courage, optimism, and determination.

In essence, constructing resilience capabilities is vital for empowering men and women to navigate life's challenges with strength, adaptability, and perseverance. By cultivating emotional regulation, problem-solving skills, nice coping mechanisms, and a boom mindset, folks can construct resilience as a core potential that allows them to thrive in the face of adversity. As we make investments in constructing resilience skills, we unencumber the viable to navigate life's challenges with resilience, courage, and resilience.

Cultivating a Positive Mindset

Cultivating a fine mind-set is a effective resilience-building method that allows persons to reframe barriers as possibilities for growth, learning, and private development. A tremendous attitude entails adopting an constructive and hopeful outlook on life, focusing on strengths, possibilities, and solutions as an alternative than residing on limitations, setbacks, or failures. By nurturing a advantageous mindset, people can domesticate resilience, beautify well-being, and navigate challenges with grace, optimism, and resilience.

One vital component of cultivating a wonderful mind-set is training gratitude and understanding for the advantages and possibilities in one's life. Gratitude includes acknowledging and savoring the advantageous components of life—such as supportive relationships, moments of joy, and private achievements—and cultivating an mindset of perception and thankfulness. By focusing on what is going nicely as a substitute than residing on what is missing or going wrong, men and women can domesticate a experience of optimism, resilience, and well-being, even in the face of adversity.

Moreover, cultivating a high-quality attitude entails reframing boundaries and setbacks as possibilities for growth, learning, and non-public development. Resilient folks view challenges as transient setbacks alternatively than insurmountable barriers, embracing adversity as a catalyst for boom and transformation. They undertake a solution-focused mindset, focusing on what they can manipulate and impact alternatively than residing on elements past their control. By reframing limitations as possibilities for boom and learning, folks can domesticate resilience and perseverance in the face of adversity.

Additionally, self-compassion is crucial for cultivating a tremendous mind-set and constructing resilience. Self-compassion entails treating oneself with kindness, understanding, and acceptance, in particular at some stage in instances of concern or failure. Resilient people exercise self-compassion by way of supplying themselves phrases of encouragement, self-care, and aid when dealing with challenges or setbacks. They understand that failure and adversity are inevitable components of the human journey and reply to themselves with compassion and empathy as a substitute than self-criticism or judgment.

Furthermore, fostering a feel of cause and that means in existence is crucial for cultivating a fine mind-set and constructing resilience. Individuals who have a clear feel of purpose—a deeply held trust in some thing higher than themselves—are higher geared up to navigate challenges with resilience and determination. They are prompted with the aid of a experience of that means and fulfillment, drawing power and resilience from their feel of motive and dedication to some thing large than themselves.

In essence, cultivating a high-quality mind-set is necessary for constructing resilience and navigating life's challenges with grace, optimism, and resilience. By practicing gratitude, reframing limitations as opportunities, training self-compassion, and fostering a feel of motive and meaning, folks can domesticate resilience as a core capability that allows them to thrive in the face of adversity. As we domesticate a tremendous mindset, we release the possible to navigate life's challenges with resilience, courage, and resilience.

Seeking Support Networks

Seeking guide networks is a fundamental issue of constructing resilience and overcoming obstacles, as it affords folks with the emotional support, encouragement, and point of view wished to navigate challenges with resilience and perseverance. Support networks embody a numerous vary of relationships, which include friends, household members, mentors, colleagues, and neighborhood groups, who provide empathy, understanding, and realistic help at some stage in instances of need.

One indispensable component of looking for help networks is recognizing the significance of social connections in promotion resilience and well-being. Strong social aid networks furnish a buffer in opposition to stress, loneliness, and adversity, imparting a feel of belonging, acceptance, and validation that fosters resilience and emotional well-being. By cultivating significant connections and nurturing supportive relationships, persons can draw electricity and resilience from their social networks, understanding that they are now not by myself in dealing with life's challenges.

Moreover, in search of help networks entails accomplishing out to others for help, guidance, and encouragement throughout hard times. Resilient persons are no longer afraid to ask for assist when needed, recognizing that looking for assist is a signal of electricity as a substitute than weakness. Whether searching for recommendation from a mentor, sharing worries with a friend, or becoming a member of a help group, achieving out to others lets in people to reap perspective, get admission to resources, and obtain the emotional assist wanted to navigate challenges with resilience and confidence.

Additionally, fostering supportive relationships entails being inclined to provide assist and help to others in their time of need. Resilient persons apprehend the reciprocal nature of social guide and are inclined to lend a listening ear, provide phrases of encouragement, or supply sensible help to friends, household members, and colleagues going through challenges. By giving and receiving help inside their social networks, men and women can domesticate a feel of reciprocity, trust, and mutual guide that strengthens resilience and fosters well-being.

Furthermore, looking for help networks includes recognizing the significance of variety and inclusion in constructing resilient communities. Resilient communities are characterized with the aid of inclusivity, empathy, and solidarity, the place people from numerous backgrounds and views come collectively to guide one some other via life's challenges. By fostering an inclusive and supportive neighborhood environment, persons can create a feel of belonging and connection that promotes resilience, well-being, and collective thriving.

In essence, looking for aid networks is imperative for constructing resilience and overcoming obstacles, as it affords people with the emotional support, encouragement, and standpoint wanted to navigate challenges with resilience and perseverance. By cultivating significant connections, attaining out for assist when needed, supplying help to others, and fostering inclusive neighborhood environments, people can construct sturdy help networks that promote resilience, well-being, and collective thriving. As we are looking for assist networks and domesticate resilience inside ourselves and our communities, we free up the manageable to navigate life's challenges with courage, strength, and resilience.

Learning from Failure

Learning from failure is a pivotal element of constructing resilience and overcoming obstacles, as it provides precious lessons, insights, and possibilities for increase and non-public development. Resilient persons view failure no longer as a remaining result or a reflection of their well worth however as a herbal section of the studying process—a stepping stone to success and resilience. By embracing failure as a instructor and a catalyst for growth, persons can extract precious lessons, insights, and knowledge that empower them to navigate challenges with resilience and determination.

One integral factor of mastering from failure is adopting a increase mindset—an mindset of curiosity, openness, and resilience closer to challenges and setbacks. Individuals with a boom mind-set view failure as an chance for boom and learning, reframing setbacks as brief setbacks instead than everlasting failures. They method failure with optimism, perseverance, and a trust in their capacity to jump returned and be triumphant in the face of adversity. By embracing failure as a herbal phase of the mastering process, men and women can domesticate resilience and perseverance in the face of adversity.

Moreover, getting to know from failure includes reflecting on one's experiences, figuring out instructions learned, and making use of them to future moves and decisions. Resilient people interact in reflective practices such as journaling, self-assessment, and comments seeking, permitting them to attain insights into their strengths, weaknesses, and areas for improvement. By reflecting on previous disasters and setbacks, men and women can become aware of patterns, root causes, and choice procedures that decorate their resilience and effectiveness in future endeavors.

Additionally, getting to know from failure includes embracing a boom mindset—an mindset of curiosity, openness, and resilience in the direction of challenges and setbacks. Individuals with a boom attitude view failure as an probability for increase and learning, reframing setbacks as transient setbacks instead than everlasting failures. They strategy failure with optimism, perseverance, and a faith in their capacity to jump again and prevail in the face of adversity. By embracing failure as a herbal section of the gaining knowledge of process, persons can domesticate resilience and perseverance in the face of adversity.

Furthermore, getting to know from failure includes in search of remarks and preparation from others who have skilled comparable challenges or setbacks. Mentors, coaches, and friends can provide precious perspectives, insights, and recommendation that allow people to obtain new insights, boost new skills, and strategy challenges with resilience and confidence. By in search of comments and coaching from others, men and women can leverage the knowledge and journey of others to navigate challenges greater efficiently and jump lower back from setbacks with resilience and determination.

In essence, getting to know from failure is crucial for constructing resilience and overcoming obstacles, as it affords treasured lessons, insights, and possibilities for boom and non-public development. By embracing failure as a herbal phase of the getting to know process, reflecting on one's experiences, searching for remarks and instruction from others, and making use of classes realized to future movements and decisions, persons can domesticate resilience as a core ability that empowers them to thrive in the face of adversity. As we examine from failure and domesticate resilience inside ourselves, we unencumber the practicable to navigate life's challenges with courage, strength, and resilience.

Chapter 10: Sustaining Productivity Momentum

Establishing Habits for Long-Term Success

Establishing habits for long-term success is foundational to sustaining productiveness momentum and accomplishing lasting consequences in each non-public and expert endeavors. Habits are automated behaviors and routines that we function regularly, frequently besides mindful thought, and they play a tremendous function in shaping our day by day actions, decisions, and outcomes. By deliberately cultivating habits that help our dreams and priorities, we can create a strong basis for long-term success and productivity.

One critical issue of organizing habits for long-term success is figuring out key behaviors and routines that align with our dreams and values. Reflecting on our priorities, aspirations, and areas for enhancement permits us to pinpoint precise habits and moves that can propel us in the direction of our preferred outcomes. Whether it is dedicating time every day for centered work, prioritizing healthful habits such as exercising and perfect nutrition, or working towards mindfulness and reflection, intentional dependency formation requires clarity, intentionality, and consistency.

Moreover, organizing habits for long-term success entails breaking down large desires into smaller, manageable moves and incorporating them into our day by day routines. By imposing gradual adjustments and incremental improvements, we can construct momentum and preserve our efforts over time. Consistency is key in dependency formation, as repeating behaviors commonly reinforces neural pathways in the brain, making them extra automated and ingrained over time. Setting specific, measurable, achievable, relevant, and time-bound (SMART) dreams can assist us remain to blame and song our development as we work closer to organizing new habits.

Additionally, growing a conducive surroundings that helps our preferred habits is crucial for long-term success. Removing limitations and distractions, developing visible cues and reminders, and surrounding ourselves with supportive assets and human beings can help strengthen our preferred behaviors and make it less difficult to continue to be on track. Building accountability mechanisms, such as sharing our dreams with a pal or becoming a member of a supportive community, can supply extra motivation and encouragement to stick to our habits even when confronted with challenges or setbacks.

Furthermore, celebrating small victories and milestones alongside the way can beef up advantageous behaviors and encourage us to proceed our efforts toward long-term success. Recognizing our progress, acknowledging our achievements, and moneymaking ourselves for assembly milestones can enhance our confidence, morale, and motivation, making it less difficult to maintain our productiveness momentum over the lengthy term. By cultivating a mind-set of development and growth, we can include the trip of addiction formation as an ongoing manner of learning, adaptation, and self-improvement.

In essence, organizing habits for long-term success is quintessential for sustaining productiveness momentum and reaching lasting effects in our non-public and expert lives. By figuring out key behaviors and routines, breaking down dreams into manageable actions, developing a supportive environment, and celebrating development alongside the way, we can construct a basis for success that endures over time. As we domesticate habits that align with our desires and values, we free up the possible to preserve productiveness momentum, gain our aspirations, and lead gratifying lives.

Overcoming Procrastination and Burnout

Overcoming procrastination and burnout is imperative for retaining productiveness momentum and stopping setbacks in our pursuit of long-term success. Procrastination, the tendency to extend or keep away from tasks, and burnout, a country of emotional, mental, and bodily exhaustion, are frequent challenges that can derail our productiveness and avert our development in the direction of our goals. By perception the root motives of procrastination and burnout and enforcing advantageous techniques to tackle them, we can maintain our productiveness momentum and thrive in our non-public and expert lives.

One imperative factor of overcoming procrastination and burnout is recognizing the underlying elements that make a contribution to these challenges. Procrastination regularly stems from worry of failure, perfectionism, overwhelm, or lack of motivation, whilst burnout can end result from persistent stress, overwork, lack of boundaries, or disengagement from significant activities. By figuring out the particular triggers and patterns that lead to procrastination and burnout in our very own lives, we can boost centered techniques to tackle them and domesticate a extra sustainable method to productivity.

Moreover, combating procrastination and burnout entails cultivating self-awareness and mindfulness to apprehend when we are falling into unproductive patterns or experiencing signs and symptoms of burnout. By tuning into our thoughts, emotions, and bodily sensations, we can perceive early warning symptoms of procrastination or burnout and take proactive steps to intervene earlier than they escalate. Practices such as mindfulness meditation, journaling, or ordinary self-reflection can assist us domesticate higher self-awareness and resilience in the face of challenges.

Additionally, imposing high-quality time administration strategies and productiveness techniques can help us overcome procrastination and stop burnout by means of growing our effectivity and focus. Breaking duties down into smaller, manageable steps, prioritizing duties primarily based on significance and urgency, and the use of strategies such as the Pomodoro Technique or time blocking off can assist us preserve momentum and keep away from feeling overwhelmed via our workload. Setting practical dreams and deadlines, organizing routines and rituals, and minimizing distractions can additionally beautify our productiveness and forestall procrastination and burnout.

Furthermore, addressing underlying problems such as perfectionism, concern of failure, or imposter syndrome can assist us overcome procrastination and construct resilience in the face of setbacks. By reframing failure as a herbal section of the mastering process, embracing imperfection, and adopting a boom mindset, we can minimize the concern and anxiousness that frequently lead to procrastination and perfectionism. Cultivating self-compassion, placing sensible expectations, and looking for guide from others can additionally assist us navigate challenges with higher resilience and self-confidence.

In essence, overcoming procrastination and burnout is fundamental for preserving productiveness momentum and attaining long-term success in our private and professional lives. By grasp the root reasons of these challenges, cultivating self-awareness and mindfulness, imposing fantastic time administration techniques, and addressing underlying issues, we can preserve our productiveness momentum, forestall burnout, and thrive in our endeavors. As we improve resilience and self-awareness, we release the achievable to overcome procrastination, stop burnout, and reap our dreams with self assurance and purpose.

Prioritizing Self-Care and Well-Being

In the pursuit of sustained productiveness momentum, prioritizing self-care and well-being is paramount. Self-care encompasses a vary of practices and things to do designed to promote physical, mental, and emotional health, nurturing our ordinary well-being and resilience. While it can also appear counterintuitive to prioritize self-care when striving for productivity, neglecting our well-being can lead to burnout, diminished productivity, and usual dissatisfaction with life.

One necessary factor of prioritizing self-care is recognizing the significance of managing stress and retaining stability in our lives. Chronic stress can take a toll on our bodily and intellectual health, compromising our potential to focus, make decisions, and function at our best. By incorporating stress administration methods such as mindfulness, meditation, deep respiration exercises, and leisure strategies into our day by day routines, we can minimize stress levels, beautify our resilience, and maintain our productiveness momentum over the lengthy term.

Moreover, prioritizing self-care includes attending to our bodily fitness via suited nutrition, exercise, and ample rest. Regular bodily pastime no longer solely boosts our power degrees and improves our temper however additionally enhances cognitive feature and productivity. Eating a balanced food plan prosperous in vitamins and staying hydrated can gasoline our bodies and minds, offering the power and vitality wanted to address day by day duties and challenges. Additionally, prioritizing relaxation and leisure is integral for recharging our batteries, stopping burnout, and preserving height overall performance tiers over time.

Additionally, prioritizing self-care entails attending to our intellectual and emotional well-being, nurturing superb relationships, and enticing in things to do that convey us pleasure and fulfillment. Taking breaks at some stage in the day to recharge, spending fine time with cherished ones, pursuing interests and interests, and practicing gratitude and self-compassion are all fundamental elements of self-care that make contributions to our general well-being and resilience. By nurturing our intellectual and emotional health, we can domesticate the resilience and internal energy wished to navigate challenges with grace and perseverance.

Furthermore, placing boundaries and working towards self-compassion are crucial components of prioritizing self-care and well-being. Learning to say no to immoderate needs and commitments, placing sensible expectations for ourselves, and setting up boundaries round our time and electricity are indispensable for defending our well-being and preserving stability in our lives. Additionally, training self-compassion includes treating ourselves with kindness, understanding, and acceptance, particularly at some stage in instances of stress or failure. By practicing self-compassion, we can domesticate resilience and soar lower back from setbacks with grace and determination.

In essence, prioritizing self-care and well-being is necessary for sustaining productiveness momentum and attaining long-term success and fulfillment. By managing stress, attending to our physical, mental, and emotional health, placing boundaries, and practicing self-compassion, we can domesticate the resilience, vitality, and internal sources wished to thrive in each our private and expert lives. As we prioritize self-care and well-being, we free up the workable to maintain productiveness momentum, acquire our goals, and lead enjoyable lives.

Setting Boundaries and Managing Work-Life Balance

Maintaining productiveness momentum requires a subtle stability between work and non-public life, making it vital to set up clear boundaries and control work-life stability effectively. In brand new hyper-connected world, the place technological know-how blurs the strains between work and private time, putting boundaries will become increasingly more indispensable to forestall burnout, preserve well-being, and maintain productiveness over the lengthy term.

One imperative factor of putting boundaries is defining clear limits round work-related tasks, responsibilities, and availability. Establishing distinctive work hours, unplugging from work-related gadgets outdoor of these hours, and speaking expectations with colleagues and supervisors can assist delineate work time from private time and stop work from encroaching on different areas of life. By placing boundaries round work commitments, persons can create house for rest, relaxation, and rejuvenation, fostering typical well-being and resilience.

Moreover, managing work-life stability entails prioritizing things to do and commitments that nourish and fulfill us backyard of work. Engaging in hobbies, spending excellent time with cherished ones, pursuing pastimes and passions, and taking part in entertainment things to do are all quintessential elements of a balanced way of life that promote well-being and forestall burnout. By allocating time and power to non-work-related pursuits, folks can recharge their batteries, beautify their creativity, and keep standpoint on what certainly things in life.

Additionally, tremendous boundary-setting includes mastering to say no to immoderate demands, requests, and commitments that detract from our well-being and productivity. Saying no assertively, respectfully, and except guilt approves men and women to prioritize their desires and commitments, preserve stability in their lives, and keep their power and center of attention for duties that align with their dreams and values. By putting clear boundaries round our time, energy, and resources, we can defend our well-being, foster resilience, and maintain productiveness momentum over the lengthy term.

Furthermore, managing work-life stability requires cultivating flexibility and adaptability in our strategy to work and life. Recognizing that stability appears distinct for anyone and might also differ relying on our circumstances, priorities, and desires permits persons to modify their boundaries and commitments accordingly. Flexibility allows folks to navigate intervals of excessive workload or non-public needs except sacrificing their well-being, allowing them to hold productiveness momentum whilst additionally attending to their desires outdoor of work.

In essence, putting boundaries and managing work-life stability are necessary for sustaining productiveness momentum and attaining long-term success and fulfillment. By organizing clear limits round work, prioritizing non-work-related things to do that nourish and fulfill us, gaining knowledge of to say no assertively, and cultivating flexibility and adaptability, we can guard our well-being, preserve stability in our lives, and maintain productiveness momentum over the lengthy term. As we prioritize work-life balance, we free up the conceivable to thrive each individually and professionally, main gratifying and significant lives.

Cultivating a Growth Mindset and Continuous Learning

Cultivating a increase mind-set and embracing non-stop getting to know are necessary techniques for sustaining productiveness momentum and reaching long-term success. A boom mindset, as coined with the aid of psychologist Carol Dweck, is the trust that our competencies and brain can be developed via dedication, effort, and learning. Individuals with a boom attitude view challenges, setbacks, and disasters as possibilities for increase and getting to know alternatively than constant boundaries or warning signs of their innate abilities.

One vital component of cultivating a increase mind-set is embracing a attitude of curiosity, resilience, and perseverance toward challenges and setbacks. Rather than viewing challenges as insurmountable obstacles, people with a increase mind-set strategy them with optimism, adaptability, and a willingness to examine from their experiences. They understand that setbacks and screw ups are herbal components of the mastering method and possibilities for increase and self-improvement.

Moreover, embracing non-stop studying is fundamental for sustaining productiveness momentum and adapting to the unexpectedly altering needs of the current world. In brand new knowledge-based economy, the place capabilities and know-how shortly emerge as outdated, lifelong mastering is critical for staying relevant, adaptable, and aggressive in the workplace. By actively in search of out new knowledge, skills, and experiences, humans can beautify their capabilities, increase their perspectives, and free up new possibilities for increase and advancement.

Additionally, cultivating a increase mind-set entails reframing setbacks and disasters as possibilities for mastering and private development. Rather than living on previous mistakes or setbacks, resilient men and women with a boom mind-set extract precious lessons, insights, and knowledge from their experiences, the usage of them as stepping stones to future success. They view failure now not as a reflection of their competencies or well worth however as a herbal phase of the gaining knowledge of system and an possibility for boom and self-improvement.

Furthermore, fostering a increase attitude includes embracing challenges and stepping outdoor of one's remedy sector to pursue new possibilities and experiences. By embracing challenges with courage, curiosity, and a willingness to learn, humans can make bigger their capabilities, advance new skills, and obtain private and expert growth. Stepping outdoor of one's alleviation sector permits folks to stretch their abilities, construct resilience, and domesticate the self assurance and adaptability wished to thrive in an ever-changing world.

In essence, cultivating a increase mind-set and embracing non-stop mastering are imperative for sustaining productiveness momentum and attaining long-term success and fulfillment. By adopting a attitude of curiosity, resilience, and perseverance toward challenges, embracing non-stop learning, reframing setbacks as possibilities for growth, and stepping outdoor of one's remedy zone, humans can free up their full achievable and thrive each for my part and professionally. As we domesticate a increase mind-set and include non-stop learning, we release the practicable to preserve productiveness momentum, attain our goals, and lead gratifying lives.

Conclusion: The Ultimate Productivity Blueprint Recap

Reflecting on Key Strategies

In this concluding segment, let's replicate on the imperative techniques unveiled for the duration of "The Ultimate Productivity Blueprint." We've delved into a plethora of strategies spanning from superb time administration to the cultivation of resilience. Each approach serves as a cornerstone, meticulously designed to beautify productiveness and propel you closer to success in each your non-public and expert life.

Throughout the book, we've got explored the artwork of studying time, uncovering strategies to optimize your schedule, prioritize tasks, and harness the strength of center of attention to expand productivity. We've navigated the terrain of intention putting and planning, dissecting methodologies to set clear objectives, create actionable plans, and execute with precision. Additionally, we've got delved into the realm of organization strategies, unveiling methods to streamline workflows, declutter spaces, and preserve order amidst chaos.

Moreover, we've got ventured into the realm of motivation and discipline, uncovering the secrets and techniques to ignite internal drive, overcome procrastination, and continue to be dedicated to our desires even in the face of adversity. And, we have delved deep into the wellspring of resilience, equipping you with the equipment to soar lower back from setbacks, domesticate a high-quality mind-set, and thrive in the midst of challenges.

As we replicate on these strategies, keep in mind that productiveness is now not purely about checking off duties on a to-do listing however about aligning your moves with your aspirations, values, and imaginative and prescient for the future. It's about fostering a harmonious stability between effectivity and effectiveness, productiveness and well-being, ambition and fulfillment.

So, as you embark on your trip armed with the insights gleaned from "The Ultimate Productivity Blueprint," I inspire you to embody these techniques wholeheartedly. Apply them with intention, adapt them to your special circumstances, and permit them to serve as guiding beacons illuminating the direction in the direction of your dreams. And remember, productiveness is now not a vacation spot however a non-stop ride of growth, improvement, and transformation.

Importance of Consistency

Consistency stands as the bedrock upon which productiveness thrives and lasting success is built. Throughout our exploration of productiveness strategies, one habitual theme has emerged: the electricity of constant action. It's no longer the occasional burst of effort or the sporadic surge of motivation that yields significant results; rather, it is the day by day dedication to small, incremental growth that paves the way for widespread achievements.

Consistency is the pressure that transforms dreams into realities, habits into 2nd nature, and desires into tangible outcomes. It's the constant drip of water that carves canyons out of rock, the continual rays of daylight that nourish seeds into towering trees. In each factor of life, from private boom to expert endeavors, consistency is the catalyst that propels us ahead and sustains our momentum over time.

Moreover, consistency breeds confidence. When we constantly

exhibit up and supply results, we construct believe in ourselves and our abilities. We advance a feel of self-efficacy—the trust that we have the energy to make a difference—and this trust will become a self-fulfilling prophecy, fueling our motivation and propelling us closer to even higher achievements.

Furthermore, consistency fosters resilience. Inevitably, we will stumble upon obstacles, setbacks, and moments of doubt alongside our journey. It's at some point of these instances of trial that our dedication to consistency serves as a lifeline, anchoring us to our dreams and guiding us thru adversity. By keeping a steadfast center of attention on our imaginative and prescient and persevering with to take small steps forward, even in the face of challenges, we domesticate the resilience essential to overcome any impediment that stands in our way.

In essence, consistency is no longer purely a virtue; it is a super-power—a pressure multiplier that amplifies our efforts and propels us toward our desires with unwavering determination. So, as you navigate the route ahead, take into account the profound have an impact on of regular action. Embrace the energy of small, day by day habits, and let consistency be your compass as you experience closer to the existence of purpose, fulfillment, and success that you envision.

Building a Supportive Environment

Central to sustaining productiveness momentum is the cultivation of a supportive environment—one that nourishes, motivates, and empowers you to thrive. Throughout our journey, we have identified the profound affect that our environment have on our productivity, well-being, and usual success. From the bodily areas we inhabit to the relationships we cultivate, our surroundings performs a pivotal position in shaping our habits, attitudes, and outcomes.

First and foremost, growing a supportive surroundings entails placing clear dreams and intentions. When we have a clear feel of path and purpose, we are higher geared up to make choices and take movements that align with our objectives. Whether it is mapping out a profession trajectory, outlining non-public aspirations, or defining priorities in quite a number areas of life, readability breeds focal point and permits us to channel our strength closer to what honestly matters.

Moreover, organizing fine routines and structures is crucial for growing a supportive surroundings that fosters productiveness and well-being. By enforcing rituals and rituals that shape our days, we can optimize our time, reduce choice fatigue, and create house for deep work and significant leisure. Whether it is a morning events that units the tone for the day ahead, a workflow that streamlines duties and processes, or an nighttime ritual that promotes leisure and restful sleep, routines grant a feel of steadiness and predictability that enhances productiveness and reduces stress.

Additionally, surrounding ourselves with supportive relationships and assets is key to retaining productivity momentum. Cultivating a community of mentors, peers, and allies who inspire, challenge, and guide us can grant useful guidance, encouragement, and accountability on our journey. Likewise, tapping into sources such as books, courses, and communities that provide knowledge, inspiration, and camaraderie can gas our increase and enlarge our horizons.

Furthermore, developing a bodily surroundings that helps productiveness and well-being is integral for sustaining momentum. Whether it is organizing your workspace for greatest efficiency, decluttering your environment to decrease distractions, or incorporating factors of nature and splendor into your surroundings to decorate creativity and inspiration, designing areas that mirror your values and priorities can have a profound influence on your productiveness and normal satisfaction.

In essence, constructing a supportive surroundings is now not simply about growing exterior stipulations conducive to productivity; it is about fostering a subculture of support, encouragement, and empowerment that nurtures your increase and improvement as an individual. So, as you proceed on your journey, take time to domesticate a supportive surroundings that honors your goals, values, and aspirations. Surround your self with people, spaces, and sources that uplift and encourage you, and let their superb affect propel you in the direction of the existence you envision.

Embracing Growth and Learning

At the coronary heart of sustained productiveness momentum lies a dedication to boom and learning—a willingness to continually evolve, adapt, and make bigger our skills in pursuit of excellence. Throughout our exploration of productiveness strategies, we have come to apprehend that the direction to success is no longer a linear one however alternatively a experience of non-stop increase and self-improvement.

Embracing boom and getting to know requires cultivating a attitude of curiosity, openness, and resilience in the direction of new experiences and challenges. It entails recognizing that failure is no longer a ultimate vacation spot however as a substitute a stepping stone to success—a precious probability to learn, grow, and refine our approach. By embracing failure as a herbal section of the getting to know process, we free ourselves from the concern of making errors and open ourselves up to new chances for increase and innovation.

Moreover, embracing increase and studying potential in search of out possibilities to make bigger our knowledge, skills, and perspectives. Whether it is thru formal education, self-directed study, or experiential learning, actively pursuing new avenues of boom approves us to continue to be in advance of the curve, adapt to altering circumstances, and release new possibilities for non-public and expert development.

Additionally, embracing increase and mastering entails surrounding ourselves with mentors, peers, and position fashions who inspire, challenge, and help us on our journey. Learning from the experiences and insights of others can supply priceless guidance, encouragement, and perspective, assisting us navigate boundaries and overcome challenges with increased ease and confidence.

Furthermore, embracing increase and getting to know requires a willingness to step outdoor of our remedy area and embody soreness as a catalyst for growth. Whether it is taking on new responsibilities, pursuing bold goals, or confronting our fears and insecurities, pushing previous our limits approves us to stretch our abilities, construct resilience, and liberate our full potential.

In essence, embracing increase and mastering is now not simply a capability to an cease however a way of life—a attitude that empowers us to always evolve, adapt, and thrive in an ever-changing world. So, as you embark on your trip closer to sustained productiveness momentum, consider to embody boom and studying as your steady companions. Cultivate a mind-set of curiosity, resilience, and openness to new experiences, and let the pursuit of information and self-improvement propel you toward the existence of purpose, fulfillment, and success that you envision.

Empowering Action

As we conclude our experience thru "The Ultimate Productivity Blueprint," it is imperative to have in mind that information barring motion is basically potential. To genuinely harness the energy of productivity, we have to empower ourselves to take consistent, purposeful motion closer to our dreams and aspirations. Action is the bridge between desires and reality—the pressure that transforms imaginative and prescient into tangible results.

Empowering motion starts with readability of cause and intentionality in our pursuits. It includes clarifying our goals, defining our priorities, and charting a path of motion that aligns with our imaginative and prescient for the future. By placing specific, measurable, achievable, relevant, and time-bound (SMART) goals, we furnish ourselves with a roadmap for success and a clear goal to purpose for.

Moreover, empowering motion requires self-discipline and dedication to comply with via on our intentions. It's about displaying up consistently, even when motivation wanes or barriers arise, and taking small, incremental steps closer to our dreams every day. By cultivating habits of consistency, perseverance, and resilience, we construct the momentum indispensable to overcome challenges and remain on course, even in the face of adversity.

Additionally, empowering motion includes embracing a boom mindset—a trust in our capability to learn, adapt, and develop via experience. It's about reframing setbacks as possibilities for gaining knowledge of and growth, instead than limitations to be prevented or feared. By coming near challenges with curiosity, optimism, and a willingness to examine from failure, we release our practicable to overcome limitations and acquire larger tiers of success.

Furthermore, empowering motion requires accountability and assist from others. By sharing our desires and growth with relied on friends, mentors, or accountability partners, we create a assist machine that holds us to our commitments and affords encouragement and preparation when needed. Surrounding ourselves with a neighborhood of like-minded people who share our aspirations and values can grant beneficial motivation and thought to preserve pushing forward, even when the going receives tough.

In essence, empowering motion is the catalyst that propels us in the direction of our desires and aspirations. It's the gas that ignites our achievable and drives us to attain new heights of fulfillment and fulfillment. So, as you mirror on the insights gleaned from "The Ultimate Productivity Blueprint," I inspire you to take decisive motion closer to your desires with confidence, determination, and purpose. By empowering your self to take consistent, purposeful action, you can free up your full achievable and create the lifestyles of purpose, fulfillment, and success that you envision.